ISBN 978-1-331-24018-1
PIBN 10162974

1 MONTH OF
FREE
READING

at

www.ForgottenBooks.com

By purchasing this book you are eligible for one month membership to ForgottenBooks.com, giving you unlimited access to our entire collection of over 700,000 titles via our web site and mobile apps.

To claim your free month visit: www.forgottenbooks.com/free162974

Similar Books Are Available from
www.forgottenbooks.com

ENGLISH LITERATURE

FROM THE BEGINNINGS
TILL AFTER
HE NORMAN CONQUES

BY

STOPFORD A. BROOKE

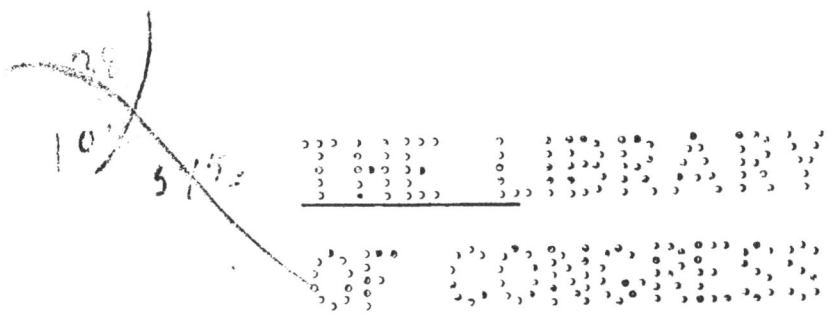

PHILADELPHIA
J. B. LIPPINCOTT COMPANY
1901

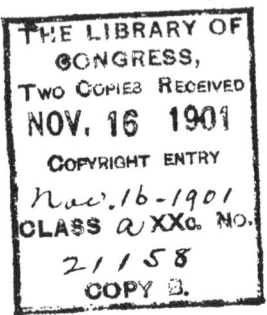
COPYRIGHT, 1901
By J. B. LIPPINCOTT COMPANY

FROM THE BEGINNINGS
TILL AFTER
THE NORMAN CONQUEST.

HE first indwellers of the islands we call Great Britain and Ireland were a wild folk, coming we know not whence, who made rude stone weapons of flint, lived by hunting, could make fires and garments of skin, and dwelt in caves. These Palæolithic people were succeeded by, or developed into, a Neolithic race whose weapons, still of stone, were now highly polished and skilfully wrought. They began pastoral life in our island, and settled finally into communities; and the large-chamber tombs under earth, or their denuded remains, extending from Caithness to Dorset, show that they occupied all the habitable parts of the country. They were a dark-haired, dark-eyed, short, brave, and constant people; and when they mingled afterwards with the Celtic race, they left some traces of their legends, religion, and law in the stories, the manners, and the language of the Celts. We may, with great probability, identify them with the earliest Picts of history, and the Silures of South Wales were their descendants.

It is only in folklore that we can hope to recover something of the way they thought and felt, but in the west of Ireland and Scotland, in Wales, and in the Midland Counties of England we still meet short, dark-haired, long-skulled people who retain the characteristics of this steady and valiant race. It is not impossible that some of the elements of their character and thought have entered into and still influence English poetry.

How long they lived undisturbed does not appear, but at last an Aryan folk, part of the first Celtic migration, invaded our island, drove back these Neolithic people to the west and north, but mingled with them, and the farther west and north they pushed the greater was the admixture. This first Celtic race are named the Goidels or the Gaels, and they colonised not only Great Britain, but also the Isle of Man, the Western Isles, and Ireland. They have lasted down to our own day, and the imaginative and enkindling spirit of their thought, literature, and art, infused into the English nature by intercourse and amalgamation, have had an intermittent and spiritual influence on the poetry and prose of England. That influence was sometimes great, as at the beginning of our literature. Sometimes it was but little, but it always inspired when it came. After King Ælfred's days, and for a very long time, it ceased to do more than now and again to touch England; but it began to act on us again at the end of the eighteenth century, and at the end of the nineteenth and beginning of the twentieth the Gaelic spirit is doing much the same kind of work it did in England during the seventh and eighth centuries.

It entered northern England from Iona, where Columba, bringing with him, and handing down to his successors, the poetry and learning of Ireland, had set up his church and dwelling. Oswald, King of Northumbria, who had been educated at Iona, summoned the Celtic monks to convert his country in 634; and Oswiu, also trained at Iona, extended the Irish influence until the whole of Northumbria received the faith from Irish missionaries, and set up a number of civilising monasteries on the Irish pattern. All the awakening and inspiring emotions of religion, out of which so much of literature is born, were kindled in the north of England at the Irish fire. This lasted untouched for thirty years; and then, alongside with the Celtic, the Latin forms of learning and religion began to make their way from Ripon, from Wearmouth, from Hexham and Jarrow. The Celtic and the Latin influences mingled. Meanwhile the Irish impulse penetrated into Mercia and East Anglia from the north; and the communication between Ireland itself and England was constant, each interchanging the results of their work and knowledge. Even the south was not exempt from the pressure of Irish wisdom. The school at Canterbury in Theodore's days was full of Irish scholars. 'Whole fleets' of students passed to and fro between Wessex and Ireland. Men like Ealdhelm were trained by Irish hermits who set up schools; and Glastonbury became a special centre of Irish learning, legend, and song; so that we may even say that Dunstan, long years afterwards, derived from the nest of Irish scholars who were settled there part of the spirit which made his character, and began that Renaissance of English learning which Ælfred had failed, but so nobly failed, to establish. This was the Goidelic invasion of England, and its imaginative and formative powers ran through all the poetry of Northumbria, and stimulated the desires of Wessex and Mercia to know, and to feel after, the unknown.

A second Wandering of the ˙Celtic race followed on the first, and some of its warriors, settling in Gaul, were allured by the white cliffs of England, and by the tales of sailors, to cross the Channel. The first of these invaders landed on the south-eastern coasts, perhaps as early as 300 B.C., and drove back the Goidels, as these had driven back the Neolithic people, to the west and north. The last of these Gaulish tribes who came to our land were the Belgæ. To all these men of the second Celtic Wandering the name of 'Brythons' has been given. When they had banished the Goidels from about a third part of Britain, the Romans checked their development for a year or two in 55 B.C., but did not come again for ninety years. During these ninety years the Brythons pushed on till they mastered the most of Britain, and even those lands where the Goidels remained (Devon, Cornwall, portions of Wales, Cumberland and Westmoreland, and part of Lancashire) became Brythonic in language, manners, and poetry. North of the Solway and the Tweed the Brythons also drove˙ their way, but with less force than in our England. They found themselves among a mixed people of Goidels and Neolithic folk in the Lowlands; and this country, sometimes Brythonic, sometimes Goidelic, ended by having in it an exceedingly mixed race, made up of these two Celtic strains dissolved in a Neolithic infusion; but the Brythonic element was master. Into the north of Scotland the Brythons scarcely penetrated. But wherever they were, their language prevailed. Later on they took the name of Cymry, and the English called them the Welsh. The fate they had given to the Goidels they met with at the hands of the English; until, after a hundred and fifty years of war, the Brythons only existed as a separate people in Devonshire, Cornwall, Wales, and in Strathclyde; that is, in the country which extended from the Ribble through Cumberland and Westmoreland to the Clyde.

The Cymry had a literature of their own, and they sang in verse the fortunes of their strife with the English, their own wars with one another, the war-deeds of their chieftains, and the tales of their families. Moreover, they made a host of stories in prose in which they embodied their myths and the legends of their ancestral heroes. Four great bards are said to have flourished among them in the later half of the sixth and the beginning of the seventh century. These were Aneurin, Taliessin, Llywarch Hen, and Merddin; and we possess in manuscripts which date from the twelfth to the fourteenth century some of their poems, added to and modernised. They sing the wars of the northern Cymry with the Angles, and of the Cymry of Wales with the West Saxons, in poems by Taliessin and Llywarch Hen. These poems are of the sixth century. In the seventh the poets celebrated the great struggle between the Northumbrians and Cadwallon and his son.

This is the first period of Cymric poetry. When the northern kingdom of the Cymry decayed, and they emigrated to South Wales, the old poetry was applied in the tenth century to the new dwelling-place and the new fortunes of the Cymry. This is the second period. Later on a third school of literature arose, poetic in North Wales, and of mythical and romantic tales in South Wales; and these tales are at the root of a great deal of English romance and song up to the present day. A fourth school of poetry, imitative of the old poetry of the north, continued under the Norman-Welsh rule till the days of Henry the Second, when the *Black Book of Carmarthen* was made up of some of the ancient poetry. In the following centuries the *Red Book of Aneurin*, the *Book of Taliessin*, and the *Book of Hergest* contained some also of the old poetry and of its later imitations. These were mingled with original work of a still later period.

There existed then, close to the border-land between the English and the Cymry, a great body of living and growing poetry, and of imaginative story-telling, which could hardly help influencing the Border-English when, after the first fierce years of the Conquest, the Welsh of West Wales, of Wales, and of Cumbria were so often either in alliance with the English or amalgamated with them. The Celtic genius of the Brythons stole in, year by year, into the English of the Border, from Berwick to Carlisle, from Carlisle to Chester, from Chester to Bristol, and from Bristol to Glastonbury and Exeter. When, after the Norman Conquest, the Normans seized a good part of South Wales, the Welsh imagination was interwoven with the

Norman passion; and in days still later, after the twelfth century, the fifth period of Welsh poetry, developing itself in lyrics of love and of nature, full of lonely and graceful sentiment, had, as I believe, a well-marked influence on the birth and growth of the earliest English lyrics. As far as we can conjecture, the best of these lyrics were born on the lands of the Severn valley, and the first English poem of imaginative importance after the Conquest—the *Brut* of Layamon—arose in the heart of one who dwelt at Areley, on the banks of the Severn.

There was no such amalgamation in the first hundred and fifty years of the conquest of Britain by the English; the British were ruthlessly slain or driven away. Among those who fled over-sea was the only literary man among the Britons whose name has attained reputation. This was Gildas, whose Latin book, *De Excidio*, describes the horrors of the first years of the English invasion, and whose *Epistola*, addressed to the kings and priests of the Britons, is a fierce and probably an exaggerated indictment of their rule and their immoralities. Nevertheless, so far as his slight history goes, he is a sound authority. When, weary of trouble he fled to Gaul, founded the Abbaye de Ruis, and died, British culture also died with him. He was not alone in his emigration. Hundreds of Britons took flight from the English sword, and out of this furious expulsion a Brythonic colony arose in France which played its own part in English literature. After the battles of Aylesford and Crayford in 455–57, and for fully a century and a half, the Britons of the southern counties and of South Wales emigrated to Armorica and made Brittany.

In that little corner of France the Brythonic traditions, legends, and myths, the imaginative ballads and story-telling of this Celtic race, lived on, and developed in freedom. When the Arthurian legend, which probably began among the northern Cymry (and the first records of which are to be found embedded in the compilation which goes under the name of Nennius—the *Historia Britonum*), came to South Wales, it got from thence into Brittany, was taken up by Breton bards, freshly worked and added to, and then fell into the hands of the Normans. The Normans, having brought to bear upon it their formative genius, carried it back to South Wales, and then to England; and it was first thrown into clear shape by a dweller in Wales, by Geoffrey of Monmouth, who composed into twelve Latin books his *History of the Britons*, which, begun in 1132, took its final form in 1147. From that day to this, for nearly eight hundred years, the Brythonic story of Arthur has been one of the master-subjects of imaginative literature in England. This—the full tale of which belongs to the next section of this book—is the last thing to be said of the influence on English literature of the Brythons, the children of the second Celtic migration.

These two Celtic invasions, the Goidelic and the Brythonic, were followed by another invasion. When the Brythons had been about four hundred years in Britain, the Romans, under Claudius, came to stay, ninety years after the invasion of Julius Cæsar in 55 B.C. Their occupation, which lasted till A.D. 410, has had no power over English literature. To some extent it had

Christianised and Romanised the Brythons; but the Roman influence did not really touch English literature till it came back with Christianity in the seventh century to England, and linked a converted people to the long traditions, literature, law, and glory of pagan and Christian Rome. But almost all the traces of this early occupation of Britain by the Romans were swept away by the hurricane of fire and sword which the English, coming in the middle of· the fifth century to conquer and to settle the land, let loose on the provincial civilisation of Britain.

English Literature
Before the English Invasion of Britain.

The first Engle-land extended from South Sweden through Denmark and its islands to the lands about the mouth of the Elbe. Its indwellers were men of three tribes—the Jutes, the Angles, and the Saxons—and their common name and tongue was English. They lived along the coast, and in their marshy settlements fought on their western shores a fierce battle with the encroaching sea; but nature was not so rough with them on the eastern coasts of Denmark. They had the expansive spirit which the sea encourages, and in their rude but seaworthy ships sailed in all weathers to ravage the neighboring coasts, terrible for courage and activity, for cruelty and greed, fearless of death and rejoicing in danger. From the Humber to Southampton they kept the British coast in terror during the later years of the Roman occupation.

Like other nations, they sang their battles at the feàst and celebrated their gods. They built up sagas of their ancestral heroes, and most of their chiefs were also bards. The older men, who did not go on piracy, farmed the lands of their settlements, and agriculture as well as war had its own songs. In these lays of religion, of war and agriculture, English poetry began in the ancient Engle-land while Britain was still a Roman province.

Of this heathen poetry on the Continent we have still some fragments left. Portions of the mythical sagas, founded on the doings of nature and of the ancestral heroes, lie embedded in *Beowulf*. The *Battle of Finnsburg* is the sole remnant of a series of sagas which were made before the time when the Folk-Wanderings began in 375. *Waldhere*, the fragment of a saga on the story of Walther of Acquitaine, carries us back to the days of the Theodoric cycle of tales. A poem entitled *Widsith* retains verses which date from the time when the English were still fighting in their lands about the Eyder and the Elbe. The *Complaint of Deor* belongs to another world than that of our island, and we possess in the scattered verses of the *Charms* which the farmer sang as he ploughed and swarmed his bees, and went on a journey and exorcised the demons of cramp and fever, perhaps the oldest remains of heathen song.

The *Charm for Bewitched Land* contains pure heathen lines such as :

Hail be thou, Earth, mother of men.
Fruitful be thou in the arms of the God.
Be filled with thy fruit for the fare-need of men.

And the rites of the ploughing which are there described are the old heathen rites of the farmer when he first drove his plough through the acre. As we have them, they are Christianised, but their pagan origin appears through the Christian recension. In the *Charm for the Swarming of Bees*, gravel is thrown over the bees, and the spell-master sings, 'Let this earth be strong against all wights whatever;' and to the bees, 'Sit ye, Victory-women, sink ye to the earth.' But the *Charm against a Sudden Stitch* is even closer to heathendom. The Charm-doctor stands over the sick man with his shield, guarding him from the darts of the Witch Maidens, and describes their ride over the hill and their flinging of spears, while he charms out the javelin which has caused the cramp. These are remnants as old as the hills, fragments from the ancient Teutonic lands before the English left them for Britain.

The earliest of the longer poems is *Widsith*, the Far-voyager. Its personal part, in which the bard tells of himself and his wanderings, may belong in its original form to the fifth century, but many additions were afterwards made to these ancient verses. Names of men much earlier and later than the fifth century were foisted in by later editors of the poem. The real interest of the verses is not in these questionable matters, but in the proud and pleasant account Widsith gives of himself as a wandering minstrel, and of the honour and gifts lavished on poets. We see him at the court of Eormanric, singing his mistress Ealdhild's praises over all lands. We hear him and his mate Scilling singing in the hall while all the lords are listening. He tells of the fighting with the Huns in the Wistla woods, and he ends by an outburst of pleasure in his art and in the honour it receives from all who care for a noble fame.

The Scôp (that is, the Shaper, the Poet), in the *Complaint of Deor*, is not so happy as Widsith. He is no rover, but lives with his lord, and has from him lands and wealth. But his rival, Heorrenda, supplants him, and this song is written to console his heart. Others, Weland, Hild, Gëat, Theodoric, suffered dreadful pain. 'This he overwent, so also will I,' is the refrain of each verse. The allusions to the sagas of Theodoric and Gudrun and Eormanric prove that the English knew, as *Waldhere* also proves, the Germanic cycle of stories. None of the examples are Christian, but the poem suffers from a Christian interpolation. It is a true lyric, with a 'refrain' at the end of each verse, and this is unique in Old English poetry.

The two fragments of the poem of *Waldhere*, found by Werlauff at Copenhagen, are made from the original German seventh-century form of the poem. The Christian and chivalric elements of the later forms are entirely absent in the verses we possess. Waldhere flies with his love Hildeguthe from the Huns, and is pursued by Guthere and Hagena. She encourages him to fight against twelve warriors in our first fragment; the second is part of the dialogue between Guthere and Waldhere.

The few lines we have of the *Fight at Finnsburg* belong to an older cycle of saga than that of Theodoric. There is another portion of this Finn-saga in *Beowulf,* and the story there told either precedes or continues our fragment. It is sung by the Scôp at the feast in Heorot, Hrothgar's hall. Finn, king of the

North Frisians, has married Hildeburh, sister of Hnæf. He invites Hnæf and his comrade Hengest, with sixty men, meaning to slay them. The verses describe the attack and defence of the hall. It is a fierce, impassioned piece of war-poetry. The related passage in *Beowulf* describes the burning of Hildeburh's sons on the pyre, and her bitter mourning for them, and the vengeance taken on Finn.

These are our heathen fragments, all of them so infiltrated with Teutonic saga that we believe that the English, when they came to our land, possessed and sang the great stories of their Continental brethren. Of other stories, both mythical and heroic, we have remains scattered through *Beowulf*—the myth of Scyld ; the story of Heremod ; the story of Thrytho, which belongs to the ancient saga of Offa ; the story of Ingeld and Froda and Freaware, which was the origin of a whole circle of tales ; and, oldest of all, the story of Sigmund, which afterwards was developed into the great *Volsunga-Saga* in the north, and in Germany into the *Nibelungen Lied*.

Beowulf.

We have one great saga of our own—the Saga of Beowulf. The poem of *Beowulf*, as we possess it, was probably composed into its present form in the eighth century in England, we do not know by whom ; and received, either then or afterwards when it was put into the West Saxon dialect, the addition, but in moderation, of certain Christian elements. The story is, however, honestly heathen, and its original lays arose on the Continent among the English. They came to our England with the Angles, were developed in Northumbria and Mercia, and may have reached full saga proportions in the seventh century. In the eighth (though some make it later) one poet took up all the scattered forms of it, wrought them into a whole, gave them an ethical unity in the character of Beowulf, the ideal hero and king, and filled the complete poem with his own personality.

Beowulf seems to have been an historical personage of the sixth century, a Geät, and nephew of Hygelac, who is the Chochilaicus whom Gregory of Tours mentions as raiding the Frisian shore, and slain by its defenders. Beowulf was present at the battle, and avenged his lord's death. Hygelac died in 520. Beowulf placed Hygelac's son on the throne, and after his death reigned fifty years. This brings the historic Beowulf up to about 570. But this historic personage has not much to do with the poem. Its main story (with folk-lore admixtures from earlier and savage times) is the transference to the hero of the mythical deeds of Beowa, who is one of the presentations of the Sun and the Summer, and whose fight with the Winter and the Darkness, with the frost-giants, the destroying sea and the poisonous mist of the moorland, imaged in the poem by the monster Grendel and the Dragon, was sung in the ancient England over the sea. The destruction of Grendel and his dam by Beowulf is said to be the destruction of the winter powers of the sea-coast as they attack one of the Danish settlements which felt alike the charging of the icy sea and the deadly cold and venom of the fenland. The story of Beowulf overcoming in his last fight the Dragon is probably the story of the aging Summer contending with the powers of incoming Winter, who attempts to grasp the treasures of the harvest. The Summer God saves the golden hoard, but dies in the struggle. These myths are embodied in the story of Beowulf, and through them his personality is built up by the poet. He becomes the English and North-Germanic ideal of a king, and the ideal is historic. The manners and customs both in war and peace, the picture of the young men sailing on adventure, the town with its hall and meadows and garths, the etiquette and feast of the hall, the daily doings of the settlement from morn to night, the position of women, the home-life, the temper of mind, the thoughts and feelings of our forefathers, are all portrayed in this poem, and there are few historical records so vivid and so interesting. It is the book of our beginnings. It is also a great sea-tale, fit for the origin of the poetry of the mistress of the seas.

Beowulf hears that Hrothgar is harried by a monster, Grendel, who haunts Heorot, the hall of the folk, and devours Hrothgar's thanes. The distressful tale thrills the hero with pity, and he sets sail to help the Danish chief. Arriving, he is told of Grendel, the man-beast of some folk-tale, the creature of the mist and the stormy sea, strong as thirty men, lonely and dreadful, greedy of blood, hating all joy, who tears and eats his victims. Beowulf and his men sleep in the hall, and Grendel, stalking over the misty moors, strikes in the doors, and rends one of Beowulf's men, but meets at last the grip of the hero. In the fierce wrestle Grendel's arm is torn away, and the monster flies through the night to die. Next morning all is happiness at Heorot ; the feast is held and gifts are given ; but at night Grendel's dam comes to avenge her son, and Hrothgar's best battle-man is torn in pieces by the wolf-woman of the sea.

This is the re-creation in a later form of the original myth—a separate and later lay. It is now woven into the poem by the single writer of the whole. Grendel's dam is a sea-monster, and lives in a sea-cave ; her hands are armed with claws ; her blood eats like fire ; she is even more savage than her son. The place where she dwells among the cliffs, in a gorge where the black waters welter furiously, is as savage as her nature ; and the description of it is the first of those natural descriptions of wild scenery of which our modern

English poetry is so full. Beowulf plunges into the sea, rises with the monster who has seized him into her cave, slays her with a magic sword, and returns triumphant with Grendel's head to Hrothgar, who sends him home to Hygelac laden with gifts and honour. This closes the first part of the poem. The second part opens some fifty years after, when Beowulf is an old man. He has been long king of the country, and his people love him. A Dragon, angry that his hoard is robbed, flies forth to burn and ravage ; and Beowulf arms to fight his last fight and to win the treasure for his folk. Only one of his thanes comes to help him, and in the battle he is wounded to the death. The Dragon is slain, the treasure is won, and the hero burned on a lofty pyre overlooking the sea.

The poem, many full accounts and translations of which have been set forth, runs to 3183 lines, and its manuscript is in the Cottonian Library in the British Museum. It has been said to be an epic, but it is more justly a narrative poem. It has neither the unity, the weight, the continuity, nor the mighty fates of an epic. Nevertheless it reaches a spiritual unity from the consistency of the hero's character developed from daring youth to wise and self-sacrificing age. It reaches even excellence in the clearness with which its portraits are drawn and its natural scenery represented. Our power of natural description in poetry begins with *Beowulf.* The verse has a fine ring in it ; the tale, if we forget the bardic repetitions, is simple, direct, and rapid ; and the spirit of it is as bold and dashing as the stormy sea near which all its actors live   Indeed, the presence and power of the sea is everywhere felt in the poem. Its close is the close of the heathen poetry of England ; for, though its composition into a whole belongs to Christian England, the lays worked up in it go back to the seventh, and some of them, it may be, to the sixth, century.

The Embarking of Beowulf.

Then the well-geared heroes
Stepped upon the stem, while the stream of ocean
Whirled the sea against the sand.   There into the ship's
    breast
Bright and carvèd things of cost, carried then the heroes,
And their armour well-arrayed.   And the men out
    pushed
Their tight ocean-wood on adventure long desired.
Swiftly went above the waves, with a wind well fitted
Likest to a fowl, their Floater, with the foam around its
    throat,

Till at last the Seamen saw the land ahead,
Shining sea-cliffs, soaring headlands,
Broad sea-nesses.   So this Sailer of the sea
Reached the sea-way's end.

Beowulf and Breca at Sea.

When we swam on the Sound, our sword was laid bare,
Hard-edged in our hands ; and against the Hron-fishes
We meant to defend us ; nor might Breca from me
Far o'er the flood-waves at all float away,
Smarter on ocean ; nor would I from him.
There we two together were tossed on the sea,
Five nights in all, till the flood apart drove us :
Swoln were the surges, of storms 'twas the coldest,
Wan waned the night, and the wind from the north,
Battling-grim, blew on us ; rough were the billows.
. . . . . . Then, eastward, came light,
Bright beacon of God ; the billows grew still.
And now I could see the sea-headlands shine,
The wind-swept rock-walls.   Wyrd often delivers
An Earl yet undoomed if his daring avail.

Half-Heathen Poetry.

Elegies and Riddles.

When the lays of *Beowulf* were made into a
poem Christianity had been long established in
England. It had come with Augustine in 597.
Its last conquest was the Isle of Wight in 686.
It took, therefore, ninety years to Christianise

England. During that interval, and indeed for a long time afterwards, a semi-heathenism prevailed. Even in Cnut's reign we find the laws forbidding the worship of heathen gods by the farmers and labourers ; and it is more than probable that the greater number of the warriors, bards, and chiefs of the seventh and eighth centuries were only Christian in name, and followed their heathen ways of thinking, feeling, and fighting. The poetry composed by the bards in a chief's following and by the wandering minstrels, outside of the monastic influence, was not likely to be influenced to any depth by Christianity. There are a few examples of such poetry in the *Exeter Book*, and five of them are of great interest—the *Ruined Burg*, the *Wanderer*, the *Seafarer*, the *Wife's Complaint*, and the *Husband's Message*. Along with these we may place a number of the *Riddles*, written, it is supposed, by Cynewulf when he was a wild young poet at some noble's court, and which treat of natural phenomena, of war and armour, of the feast and the hall of the folk, of daily life in the settlements, of hunting and cattle, of forest and fish and bird.

The first five poems mentioned above may fairly be called elegiac. They are full of regret for the glory of the past and the sadness of the present, and though we have no means of dating them, I should be inclined to place them in the first quarter of the eighth century. They are devoid of Christian sentiment and doctrine. The prologue and epilogue-of the *Wanderer*, and the long tag added to the *Seafarer*, are Christian, but these are additions quite out of harmony with the body of the poems. Where they were written is also unknown. Some allot them to the south of England and to the ninth century, others to Mercia. I believe them to be Northumbrian, and to belong to the beginning of the eighth century. Their scenery is northern, their temper is northern ; and even the *Ruined Burg*, which mourns in solemn verse the vanished glory of a desolate city, and is probably a description of the ruins of Bath, may have been written by a Mercian poet educated in the Northumbrian schools. ' Their most remarkable quality, independent of their heathen dwelling on Fate rather than on the will of God, is their love of Nature—and this too has a heathen tinge. They scarcely touch those softer aspects of the earth and sea and sky which poetry distinctly Christian loved to describe. They dwell on the tempest and the fury of the waves, on the hail lashing the broken fortress, on the thunder of the ice and the deathfulness of the snow, on the black caves in the forest and the cliffs white with the frost. There are half-a-dozen of the *Riddles* concerned with the terrible play of Nature in the northern seas, in the storm-wearied sky, and in the wild marsh and forest land. Our Nature-poetry of the nineteenth century is a reversion to this early English temper, and poetry of this kind in the eighth or the ninth century is unique in Teutonic literature of that time. Poetry of natural description is to be found also in Welsh and Irish song, and it is probable that the writing of it in England is to be traced to the influence on Northumbria and Mercia of the Celtic poets. But I also believe—and the fact that the form of the English Nature-poetry of this time is finer than any Celtic work of the kind may be due to this —that these northern poets were well acquainted with Virgil ; moreover, neither in Irish nor Welsh poetry of this period are there poems, such as the three *Riddles* on the storms, which treat of Nature alone, of Nature for her own sake. One of these is placed among the extracts. The finest of them is a long poem upon the Hurricane, impersonated as a giant rising from his prison under the earth to work his terrors on land and sea and in the sky ; and in each of these realms it is described with so much force, fire, and imagination that we know the poet had watched from point to point the actual thing.

Of the Elegies the *Wanderer* is the best, but the *Seafarer* is the most interesting. The *Wanderer* describes the mournful fates of men, the ruin of great towns and earls, friendships lost, departed glory, the winter night and snow settling on the world and on the heart of man. The *Seafarer* is perhaps a dramatic dialogue between an old and a young sailor, each telling of their terrible days at sea, yet each confessing the wild fascination of a sailor's life. The *Husband's Message*, or rather the *Lover's Message*, calls, in exile, on the sweetheart of the writer to join him in the foreign land where he waits for her : 'Come in the spring, when the cuckoo calls from the cliff.' The *Wife's Complaint* tells of her banishment by false tongues from her lord, and mourns her fate from the cave in the wood where she dwells, but mourns the most because she knows he loves her still, and suffers from want of her tenderness. These two last poems are the only poems in Old English which touch upon the passion and subtlety of human love. There may have been many more, but all the poetry of which we have to speak in the next section was written under the shadow of the monasteries, and the subject of love is absent.

The Last Verses of the 'Wanderer.'

Whoso then these ruined Walls wisely has thought over,
And this darkened life of man deeply has considered,
Sage of mood within, oft remembers, far away,
Slaughters cruel and uncounted, and cries out this
    Word—
'Whither went the horse, whither went the man?
    Whither went the Treasure-giver?

What befell the seats of feasting? Whither fled the joys
    in hall?
O, alas, the beaker bright ! O, alas, the byrnied warriors !
O, alas, the people's pride ! Ah, how perished is that
    Time !

Veiled beneath Night's helm it lies, as if it ne'er had
    been !'
Left behind them, to this hour, by that host of heroes
    loved,
Stands the Wall, so wondrous high, with Worm-images
    adorned !
Strength of ashen spears snatched away the Earls,
Swords that for the slaughter hungered, and the Wyrd
    sublime !
See, the storms are lashing on the stony ramparts ;
Sweeping down, the snow-drift shuts up fast the Earth
Woe and winter-terror when it wan ariseth ;
Darkens then the dusk of Night, from the nor'rard
    driving
Heavy drift of hail for the harm of heroes.

All is full of trouble, all this realm of Earth !
Doom of weirds is changing all the world below the
    skies ;
Here our fee is fleeting, here the friend is fleeting,
Fleeting here is man, fleeting is the Kinsman !
All the Earth's foundation is become an idle thing.

The Plough—Riddle xxii.

Nitherward my neb is set, deep inclined I fare ;
And along the ground I grub, going as he guideth me
Who the hoary foe of holt is, and the Head of me.
Forward bent he walks, he, the warden at my tail ;
Through the meadows pushes me, moves me on and
    presses me,
Sows upon my spoor.   I myself in haste am then.

Green upon one side is my ganging on ;
Swart upon the other surely is my path.

The Nightingale—Riddle ix.

Many varied voices voice I through my mouth.
Cunning are the notes I sing, and incessantly I change
    them.
Clear I cry and loud ; with the chant within my head ;
Holding to my tones, hiding not their sweetness.
I, the Evening-singer old, unto earls I bring

Bliss within the burgs, when I burst along
With a cadenced song.   Silent in their dwellings
They are sitting, bending forwards.   Say what is my
    name.

The Iceberg—Riddle xxxiv.

Came a wondrous wight o'er the waves a-faring,
Comely from his keel called he to the land.
Loudly did he shout, and his laughter dreadful was,
Full of terror to the Earth ! Sharp the edges of his
    swords,
Grim was then his hate.   He was greedy for the
    slaughter,
Bitter in the battle work ; broke into the shield-walls,
Rough and ravaging his way ; and a rune of hate he
    bound.
Then, all-skilled in craft, he said, about himself, his
    nature—
' Of the maiden kin is my mother known ;
Of them all the dearest, so that now my daughter is
Waxen up to mightiness.'

Cædmon and the Christian Poetry.

The distinctive Christian poetry begins before the date of the Elegies and the Nature-Riddles—in the seventh century, with Cædmon of Whitby.   He is the first English poet whose name we know, and it stands at the head of the long and glorious muster-roll of English singers.   We have worn Apollo's laurel for 1200 years.   Cædmon began to make verse, we may fairly say, between 660 and 670.   We know the date of his death—680 ; and we are told that he was somewhat advanced in years when the gift of song came upon him.   We first find him as a secular attendant of the monastery of Hild, an abbess of royal blood, who had set up her house of God on the lofty cliff which rises above the little harbour where the Esk meets the gray waters of the German Ocean.   Whitby is its Danish name ; in the days of Bæda it was called Streoneshalh.   Cædmon was born a heathen if he was English ; but if, as some think from his

name, he was a Celt, he was born a Christian
The monastery in which he afterwards became a
monk was founded on the Celtic pattern—one of
the children of Iona—and he was early imbued
with the Celtic spirit. Existing Celtic hymns, such
as Colman's, may have been placed before him
by the Irish monks as models for his poetry.
But, for all this, his tongue was English and
his poems were made in English. Whatever the
Irish spirit did for him, the ground of his work
was English.

Bæda tells the story of Cædmon's birth as a
poet. One night, having the care of the cattle, he
fell asleep in the stable, and One came to him and
said, 'Cædmon, sing me something.' 'I know not
how to sing,' he replied, 'and for this cause left I
the feast.' 'Yet,' said the divine visitant, 'you must
sing to me.' 'What shall I sing?' said Cædmon.
'Sing,' the other replied, 'the beginning of created
things.' And immediately Cædmon began a hymn
in praise of the World's Upbuilder, and awakening,
remembered what he had sung, and told the Town-
Reeve of his gift, who brought him to Hild; and,
becoming a monk, he continued in the abbey till
he died with joy and in peace, singing, day by
day, all the Scripture history, and of the Judg-
ment-day. 'Others after him,' said Bæda, 'tried
to make religious poems, but none could compare
with him.'

His poetry had then made a school which was
doing similar work to his when Bæda, fifty
years after Cædmon's death, was finishing his
Ecclesiastical History. Of what kind that work
was we have no certain knowledge. The
poems attributed to Cædmon by Junius in the
manuscript called the *Junian Cædmon* have been
assigned by critics to different writers. Only one
of them—*Genesis A*—is thought by a few to be
possibly from his hand. If so, he wrote the thing
in two distinct manners—partly in a mere paraphrase of the Biblical story, dull, unilluminated

by any imagination ; and partly in imaginative
episodes, in which the Fall of the rebel angels,
the Flood, the battles of Abraham, and the
story of Hagar and of Isaac are imaginatively
treated as heroic tales, in the manner of a
heathen saga, and with English feeling. It is
to be hoped that some day we shall get evidence
to prove that these fine, bold episodes are from
Cædmon's hand. The only verses we know to
be his are transferred into Latin by Bæda, and
we have a Northumbrian version of them in an
old MS. of the *Historia Ecclesiastica.* They are
the short hymn which he is said to have sung
on awakening from his dream. Their hymnic form
suggests to critics that Cædmon's work was mainly
a series of heroic hymn-like lays on the subjects of
the Old and New Testament, tinged with the colours
of the Nature and the hero myths. It may be that
we have the remains of one of these in the poem,
portions of which are carved in runic letters on the
Ruthwell Cross in Dumfriesshire. The lines sing of
'Jesus, the young Hero, who was God Almighty,
who girded Himself and stepped up, full of courage,
on the gallows for the sake of man.' And as He lies
there, the Sacred Rood speaks : 'Lifted on high, I
bore the Lord of the heavenly realm, and trembled,
all besteamed with blood. Pierced with spears and
sore pained with sorrows, I beheld it all. They laid
Him, limb-wearied, in the grave.' If this fragment
be really Cædmon's work, it fills us with deep regret
that we have lost his other poems—lost a poetry so
close to the heroic manner, so filled with the spirit
of that heathen vigour and passion which his life
had seen and known. At any rate, we owe him a
great debt. He bridged the river between the
pagan and the Christian poetry. He showed to his
folk how the new material of Christianity could be
used by the bards of England. He made a great
school of poetry. He made Cynewulf possible.
He is the first English poet in our England. The
royal line of England goes back to Cerdic, the still

more royal line of English poets goes back to Cædmon.

The poetry of the School of Cædmon belongs to the end of the seventh and the beginning of the eighth century. Some of these poems are in the *Exeter Book*. They are short hymnic songs of praise. There is the *Song of the Three Children*, adapted in the seventh century from the *Apocrypha;* and following it, the *Prayer of Azarias*. These were joined together, and furnished in later times with a conclusion, celebrating the deliverance of the three children. As the capacity for writing poetry grew, other forms were developed—poems of a half-epic character, and narrative poems with episodes like heathen lays inserted on a background of narrative. Of these two kinds of poetry, which ran together, the *Exeter Book* contains three—*Genesis A*, *Exodus*, and *Daniel;* and in the manuscript which contains *Beowulf* there is another—*Judith*. These probably belonged to Northumbria. Whether any long poems were written in the middle and south of England at this time we do not know; but we do know that the family lay and the war-song were made and sung everywhere, and we have a pleasant story which tells how Ealdhelm, Bishop of Sherborne, who died in 709, was accustomed on his preaching tours to stand like a gleeman on the bridge or the public way, and to sing songs, it may be his own, to the people flocking to the fairs, that he might draw them to him to hear the Word of God. This is the only thing we know of poetry in the south of England at this time.

Genesis A is in the Junian manuscript. This manuscript was found by Archbishop Ussher, and sent by him to Francis Du Jon (Junius), who printed it at Amsterdam some time after 1650, and published it as the work of Cædmon, because its contents and its beginning agreed with Bæda's account of Cædmon's work. It is now at the Bodleian, and is a small folio of 229 pages, in two handwritings, the first of the tenth century, and illustrated with rude pictures. The first contains the *Genesis*, the *Exodus*, and the *Daniel;* the second the poems and fragments of poems generally classed under the title of *Christ and Satan.* The *Genesis* is now divided into two parts, called *A* and *B;* and *Genesis B* and the *Christ and Satan* are now placed by the critics in the ninth and tenth centuries.

Genesis A is the first of the three poems belonging to the Cædmon School. It consists of the first 234 lines of the *Genesis,* and of the lines from 852 to the close. [The lines between 234 and 852 are *Genesis B.*] The early poem has many archaic elements, drawn from Teutonic ideas of the universe — ancient Nature-myths. Its account of Abraham's war is alive with heathen lust of battle and vengeance ; and Abraham and his comrades speak like an English earl and his thanes in counsel. When the poet comes to gentler matters the spirit of the poem is changed. The Christian sentiment for soft landscape, its love of animals, and its tender domestic feeling touch the verse, in a pathetic mingling, with grace and delicacy. The account of the Creation tells of the Hollow Chasm, black in everlasting night—the vast Abrupt that was before the earth and stars were made ; then of the birth of ocean and of light, and of Day flying from the Dark, and of Morning striding over earth and repelling the Night ; then of Man's creation, and of the winsome water washing the happy lands, and of earth made lovely with flowers—and the lines are full of the new kindliness which, unlike the heathen poetry, loved the beauty and softness of the earth and sky. Mere paraphrase follows, and then the poetic work is again taken up in the episode of the Flood, which is told by one who had seen the rain of tempest and heard the sounding of the sea, and, it may be, from the height of the abbey cliff, watched the sailors drive their barks into the harbour. Another weary piece of paraphrase brings us to Abraham's story, his visit to Egypt, his war with the kings of the East, Hagar's deliverance, and the sacrifice of Isaac. The episode is well invented, and developed with great freedom from its original. The war is English war. Abraham acts and talks like an English earl ; the raid of the Eastern kings is like a raid of the Picts into Northumbria ; the tie of comradeship between Abraham and Aner, Mamre and Eshcol, is the same as that between Beowulf and his thanes, between Byrhtnoth and his followers ; the joy in the vengeance taken is fiercely northern. ' No need,' cries Abraham, ' to fear any more the fighting rush of the Northmen. The carrion-birds, splashed with their blood and glutted with their corpses, are sitting now on the ledges of the hills.' Dialogue, which belongs to the whole of the episodes and gives them life and movement, is largely used in the story of Hagar, and almost suggests the drama. The sacrifice of Isaac is full of Teutonic touches—the bale-fire, the white-haired gold-giver girding his gray sword on him, the sun stepping upwards, the high wolds where the pyre is made, the vivid reality of a Northman's human sacrifice ; and the poem ends with the cry of God : ' Pluck the boy away living from the pile of wood.'

The *Exodus* is a complete whole. It is not troubled by paraphrase. The writer uses the greatest freedom with his subject, inventing, expanding, elaborately exalting his descriptions ; beginning with the death of the first-born, and ending with the triumph over Pharaoh. War and the array of battle give him great pleasure. He describes Pharaoh's host on their march with vigour and fire ; and the marshalling of Israel before the passage of the sea is full of poetic pleasure. In both passages, what an English host was like at the beginning of the eighth century is exactly detailed. The great war, however, is the war of

God against the Egyptians, His menace of their host on the march, His use against them of the blackness of tempest, the charging waves, the bloody flood. These were God's ancient swords. Many times the poet describes the overwhelming. It is forcible—over forcible; but young poetic life is in it. And the poem closes with the Song of victory and the plunder of the dead Egyptians.

Judith, in the manuscript which contains *Beowulf*, is probably of the same cycle as the *Exodus*—a poem of the middle of the eighth century. Like the *Exodus*, the poem is conceived as a Saga, to be sung before the warriors in camp as well as the monks in the refectory. It seems to have been in twelve books, for our manuscript contains a few lines of Section ix., and the whole of Sections x., xi., and xii. Section x. begins with the feast of Holofernes and the leading of Judith to his tent. He reels into his bed, drunken and shouting. 'Avenge, O God!' she cries, 'this burning at my heart;' and the slaughter of the heathen chief is told with accurate delight. Book xi. brings us to Bethulia. Judith calls on all the burghers to arm for battle, and again English war is described. The warriors, bold as kings, run swiftly to the carnage, showers of spears fall on the foes, and the sword-play is fierce among the doomed. The gaunt wolf, the raven, and the dusky eagle rejoiced on that day. The twelfth book tells of the surprise of the Assyrian host, their flight, and the gathering of the spoil; and Judith ends it with the praise of God. She towers over the whole, a noble and heroic figure, fit to receive and wear her spoil—the sword and helm, war-shirt and gems, of Holofernes.

The *Daniel* closes this earliest cycle of Christian poetry. It has no literary quality—a mere monkish paraphrase of the book as far as the feast of Belshazzar. The school of Cædmon had reached its decay.

The poetry of that school took its materials from the Old Testament. Christ was celebrated in it as the Creator, the great warrior who overthrew the rebel angels, the Egyptians, the Assyrians. It was eminently English ; it was eminently objective. The personality of the poet does not intrude into the poems.

The second school of Christian poetry is clearly divided from its predecessor. Cynewulf was its founder and its best artist. Its subjects are drawn from the New Testament and the martyr stories and legends of the Church of Rome. It is more Latin in feeling than English. Christ is celebrated, not as the God of the Jews who destroys His foes, but as the Saviour of the world of men for whom He dies, and the Judge who is to come. The note of it is a note of sorrow on the earth, but of joy to be in heaven. In the life to come is the rapture which fills the hymns of Cynewulf. And, finally, the poetry almost ceases to be objective. The personal passion of the poet enters into every subject, and runs like a river through every poem. Even the natural description is touched with its colour.

Abraham's Battle with the Elamites.

So they rushed together. Loud were then the lances,
Savage then the slaughter-hosts. Sadly sang the wan fowl,
All her feathers dank with dew, 'midst the darting of the shafts,
Hoping for the corpses. Then the heroes hastened
In their mighty masses, and their mood was full of thought.

Hard the play was there,
Interchanging of death-darts, mickle cry of war !
Loud the clang of battle ! With their hands the heroes
Drew from sheath their swords ring-hilted,
Doughty of the edges.

               In the camps was clashing
Of the shields and shafts, of the shooters falling ;
Brattling of the bolts of war ! Underneath the breast
    of men
Grisly gripped the sharp-ground spears
On the foemen's life. Thickly fell they there
Where, before, with laughter, they had lifted booty.
                      (*Genesis*, ll. 1982–2060.)

The Approach of Pharaoh.

               Then they saw
Forth and forward faring, Pharaoh's war array,
Gliding on, a grove of spears ; glittering the hosts !
Fluttered there the banners, there the folk the march
    trod.
Onwards surged the war, strode the spears along,
Blickered the broad shields ; blew aloud the trumpets.
Wheeling round in gyres, yelled the fowls of war,
Of the battle greedy ; hoarsely barked the raven,
Dew upon his feathers, o'er the fallen corpses ;
Swart that chooser of the slain ! Sang aloud the wolves
At the eve their horrid song, hoping for the carrion.
Kindless were the beasts, cruelly they threaten ;
Death did these march-warders, all the midnight through,
Howl along the hostile trail—hideous slaughter of the
    host.

Cynewulf.

Cynewulf, with whom the second period of Old
English poetry begins, was, in the opinion of a
large number of critics, a Northumbrian, but some
think him to have been Mercian. It is difficult
to conceive how a poet so well acquainted with
the sea and the coasts of the sea should have
written in Mercia. A Mercian might have been
acquainted with the sea, but not impassioned by
it, as Cynewulf proves he is. Moreover, the sadness of his poetry, the constant regret for vanished
glory, does not suit the life in Mercia at this time,
when, from 718 to 796, Æthelbald and Offa had
made Mercia the greatest kingdom in England ;
but does suit the life in Northumbria when, from

750 to 790, that kingdom had fallen into anarchy and decay. There are other critics who place him much later than the eighth century.

We know the name of the poet, and something of his life and character. He has signed his name in runic letters to four of his poems. His riddling commentary on these runes gives personal details of parts of his life. His youth, he says, 'was radiant.' He was sometimes attached as a Scôp to a chieftain; sometimes he played the part of a wandering singer. He had received many gifts for his singing, then fallen into need; had known the griefs of love, and lived the wild life of a young poet; so that, when looking back on his youth, he thinks of himself as stained with many sins. Then the scenery of his life changed. Some heavy misfortune fell on him, and he tells us then that his repentance was deep. In his sorrow for sin he had a vision of the Cross, and felt the blessing of forgiveness. His 'gift of song' that he had lost in his remorse and fear returned to him, and then he began to write his Christian poetry. In that poetry we read his sensitive, im-passioned, self-contemplative character. He is as personal as Milton or Cowper; but, unlike Cowper, he passes from religious sorrow into religious peace, and the poems written in his old age are full of contented aspiration for the better kingdom.

The *Riddles*, it is generally understood, contain a great deal of his early work before his con-version. If they are his, they tell us that he knew some Latin and had lived in monasteries, probably as a scholar; was a lover of natural scenery, of animals and birds; was eager in the works of war, and had sung the sword, the spear, the war-shirt, and the bow; had watched with an observant eye the village and the town on the edge of the woods, the river, the mill, the loom, the gardens, the domestic animals. Moreover, he had seen and described, with a young man's joy in the tempest, the cliffs and shore white with the leaping waves, the ships labouring in the mountainous sea, the folk-halls burning in the gale, the woods ravaged by the lightning and the black rain. All this and much more is celebrated in the *Riddles*. With his love of impersonation, he personified far more than his riddle-making predecessors, Ealdhelm, Symphosius, and Tatwine, the subjects of his enigmas. When he makès the Iceberg ride like a Viking over the waves, and charge, breaking his enemies' ships, with fierce singing and laughing, to the shore, we feel that he could scarce carry further imaginative personation of natural phenomena. Yet he is so particular in observation of Nature that he devotes three separate *Riddles* to the description of three several kinds of tempest, and they are done with imaginative intensity, nor is the phrase exaggerated.

The *Riddles* are in the *Exeter Book*, in three divisions. There are ninety-five of them, but these are combined into eighty-nine. There were probably a hundred. Those written by Ealdhelm and others before Cynewulf's time were in Latin ; these are in English verse, with the exception of the eighty-sixth, which is in Latin. As the name Lupus is in it, it is supposed that Cynewulf thus recorded his name.

When we meet Cynewulf again he is all changed. He has suffered sore trouble, and is overwhelmed with sorrow for sin ; and we possess, mingled up with the runes of his name, his record of misery in the *Juliana*, the first, probably, of his signed poems. Here, as an example both of the fashion of his signature and of his penitence, is the passage

> Sorrowful are wandering
> C and Y and N ; for the King is wrathful,
> God of conquests giver. Then, beflecked with sins,
> E and V and U must await in fear
> What, their deeds according, God will doom to them
> For their life's reward. L and F are trembling,
> Waiting, sad with care.

The *Juliana* is in the *Exeter Book*, and Cynewulf has worked up the legend of this virgin and
martyr in a series of episodes so abrupt, so full
of repetition, with so awkward a hand, that it
plainly suggests a beginner's work in a new
method. From a wild young poet to a sad peni-
tent, from versing of war and love and nature to
versing a pious legend, are not transitions which
are easily made, nor is the work done in such a
transition imaginative. We may say the same of
the first part of the *St Guthlac*, which he has
not signed, but which we think was written in this
transition period. It rests on traditions of the
saint, and is a lifeless piece of writing.

In the *Crist*, which is the next signed poem,
Cynewulf has passed through this transition time,
and attained ease, life, and eagerness in his art ;
recovered his imaginative power, his passion, and
his descriptive force. Here, for the first time in
his Christian work, he reaches originality, his true
method and fit material. The *Crist* is not the
translation of a legend ; it is freshly invented ;
and Cynewulf is always at his best when he
is inventing, not imitating. The sorrow for his
sinful life continues, but it is now mingled with
the peace which comes of realised forgiveness. ' I
have sailed on wind-swept seas,' he cries, ' over
fearful surges, but now my ship is anchored in
the haven to which the Spirit-Son of God has
brought me home.'

The *Crist* is in the *Exeter Book*. It was scattered
in fragmentary pieces through this book, but has
now been brought together. It consists of three
parts. The first celebrates the Nativity, the second
the Ascension, the third the Day of Judgment, and
the poem closes at line 1663. The series of can-
tatas into which the first part is set are remarkable
not only for the rushing praise with which each of
them ends, but also for a dramatic dialogue, almost
like the dialogue in the Miracle-Plays, between a
choir of men and women from Jerusalem and Mary

and Joseph. It reads like a prediction of the medieval mysteries. In the second part there is a finely conceived scene, set in the vast of space, of Christ returning to His Father's home, leading all the Old Testament saints up out of Hades, and of the meeting with Him and them of the host of heaven who have poured from the gates to welcome the new-comers. The third part of the poem begins with the gathering of the angels and the saints on Mount Zion. A noble description follows of the Angels of the four trumpets summoning the dead. Christ appears in a blazing light, and the universe melts in conflagration. Only Mount Zion remains, and the throne, and the dead, small and great, before it. Then, with its root on the mount and its top in heaven, a mighty Cross is upraised, wet with the blood of the King, but so brilliant that all shade is drowned in its crimson light. This fine conception is Cynewulf's own, and in its description, and in that of the great conflagration, the power he showed in the *Riddles* reaches its highest point. The poem ends with a picture of the saints in the perfect land.

The *Crist* was followed by the *Phœnix* and the second part of the *Guthlac*. Neither of these are signed by Cynewulf, but the majority of scholars allot them to him. The *Phœnix* is in the *Exeter Book*, and its source is a Latin poem by Lactantius. This original is left at line 380; the rest is an allegory of the Resurrection, in which not only Christ but all the souls of the just are symbolised by the rebirth of the Phœnix. The first part describes the paradisiacal land—the equivalent of the Celtic land of eternal youth—in which the Phœnix dwells, and the description is famous in Old English work. Then the enchanted life of the bird is told with all Cynewulf's love of animals, of lovely woodland places, of the glory of the sunrising and the sunset, and of sweet singing; and then the flight of the bird to the Syrian land, its burning, its resurrection, and the return to its Paradise for another thousand years. The allegory follows. It is plain from the joyousness, the exultation of this poem, and its rapturous praise, that Cynewulf had fully recovered from his spiritual misery, and was happy in faith and hope.

The second part of *Guthlac*, which Cynewulf now added, as I think, to the first part, has for its subject the death of Guthlac, and is told in the manner of the saga stories. I have conjectured that Cynewulf, who in the previous poems had avoided the heroic and mythical terms of the heathen poetry, as he would be likely to do after his conversion from a life he held in horror, now felt his religious being so firmly set that he allowed himself to recur to the poetic fashions of his youth. At any rate, in this poem and in the later poems he sings the Christian battle with death, the victory of Jesus over evil, the legends of the Church, with a full use of the old heroic strain, of the Nature-myths, and of the terms of heathen war. Guthlac stands on his hill, like a Viking, as if on Holmgang, to meet the assaults of Satan and his 'smiths of sin;' to stand against Death, that greedy warrior; and dies in triumph. A pillar of light rises from his corpse, and the heavenly host bursts into rapturous singing to welcome him. All England trembles with joy. It is an unfinished poem, but there is no better work in Old English poetry.

A fragment of a *Descent into Hell* also belongs to this poet, and is written with the same trick of dialogue and the same enthusiasm as the *Crist*, and in the same heroic manner as the *Guthlac*. This poem also is not signed.

There are two signed poems yet to be spoken of, and two unsigned, which many critics have allotted to Cynewulf. The two signed poems are the *Fates of the Apostles* and the *Elene*. The two unsigned are the *Andreas* and the *Dream of the Rood*. No discussion has gathered round the *Elene*. It is plainly Cynewulf's. A great deal of discussion has gathered round the *Dream of the Rood*. Again and again it has been claimed for Cynewulf; again and again the claim has been denied. The same may be said with regard to the *Andreas*. As to the *Fates of the Apostles*, most people think the signature makes it plainly his; but the date of its production and whether it stands alone or is an epilogue to the *Andreas* are matters still in discussion. The best thing this short treatise can do is to leave these critical matters, and to speak of the poems themselves. If the *Fates of the Apostles* be bound up with the *Andreas*, and if Cynewulf wrote the *Andreas*, it is here, after the second part of *Guthlac*, that we may best place these poems.

The *Fates of the Apostles* is in the *Vercelli Book*, and the personal passage (if it really belong to that poem) contains Cynewulf's name. The work of the apostles is told as if it were the expedition of English Æthelings against their foes. 'Thomas bore the rush of swords; Simon and Thaddeus were quick in the sword-play.' This heroic cry is equally strong in the *Andreas*; but the manner of the whole poem does not resemble the other work of Cynewulf. It has many lines which recall *Beowulf*, and the writer seems to have read that poem. If it is by an imitator of Cynewulf, the imitator was capable of as good work as Cynewulf; and he loves the grim sea-coasts and the stormy sea as much as Cynewulf. It would be pleasant to think that there were two such good men at this time writing together.

The *Andreas* is in the *Vercelli Book*, and tells from the *Acts of St Andrew and St Matthew*, of which there is a Greek manuscript at Paris, the adventures of the two apostles among the Mermedonians, a cannibal Ethiopian tribe. The apostles, the angels, even Christ Himself, are all English in speech, and the scenery is English. There is, of course, nothing English in the original. The change is a deliberate addition made by

the writer. As literature, the important part of
the poem is the voyage of St Andrew and his
thanes with Christ and two angels, their conversa-
tion, the description of the storm, their landing on
the coast. All this is done in heroic fashion ; the
breath of the sea fills it ; the natural description
is terse and observant, and the talk is imaginatively treated. We feel as if we were sailing in
a merchant-boat of the eighth century between
Whitby and the Tyne. Landing, Andrew delivers
Matthew, suffers three days' martyrdom, and then,
after a mighty flood and tempest of fire has
destroyed his foes, converts the rest, founds a
church, and sails away.

There is no doubt of the authorship of the
Elene, which Cynewulf wrote when he was 'old
and ready for death in my frail tabernacle.' It
is the last of the signed poems. He was now a
careful artist. 'I've woven craft of words,' he
says, 'culled them out, sifted night by night my
thoughts.' He then recalls the story of his life
while he signs his name in runes. It is the chief
biographical passage in his work, and it ends with
a fine description of the storm-wind hunting in
the sky. The poem is in the *Vercelli Book*—
1320 lines. The subject is the Finding of the
True Cross by the Empress Helena. The battle
of Constantine with the Huns and the voyage of
Helena are the best parts of the poem. They
are insertions by Cynewulf into the Latin life of
Cyriacus, Bishop of Jerusalem, which (in the *Acta
Sanctorum*, May 4) is the source of the poem.
The battle is done with the full heroic spirit. The
sea-voyage breathes of his delight in the doings or
ships and of the ocean. The ancient saga-terms
strengthen and animate his verse, and the poet
seems to write like a young man. His metrical
movement is steadier here than in the other poems.
He uses almost invariably the short epic line into
the usage of which English poetry had now drifted.
Rhyme, also, and assonance are not infrequent.

The poets, it is plain, had now formulated rules for their art. Had Northumbrian poetry lasted, it might have become as scientific as the Icelandic.

The last poem belonging to Cynewulf or his school is the *Dream of the Rood*, which is found in the *Vercelli Book*. Its authorship is unknown, but many scholars give it to Cynewulf. I believe it to be his last poem, his farewell ; and that he worked it up from that early 'Lay of the Rood' written, it is supposed, by Cædmon, and a portion of which is quoted on the Ruthwell Cross. Cynewulf wished to record before he died the vision of the Cross which converted him. He found this poem of Cædmon's, and wrought it up into a description of his vision, inserting the 'long epic lines' in which it was written. Then he wrote a beginning and end of his own in his 'short epic' line. This theory—it is no more—accounts for the difficulties of the poem

It begins by describing how he saw at the dead of night a wondrous Tree, adorned with gems, moist with blood ; and how, as he looked on it, heavy-hearted with sin, it began to tell its story.

I was hewed down in the holt, and wrought into shape, and set on a hill, and the Lord of all folk hastened to mount on me, the Hero who would save the world. Nails pierced me ; I was drenched with the Hero's blood, and all Creation wept around me. Then His foes and mine took Almighty God from me, and men made His grave, and sang over Him a sorrowful lay.

The old poem, thus worked up into Cynewulf's new matter, may be distinguished by its long epic lines from the newer matter, which is written in the short epic line. When the dream is finished, Cyne-wulf ends with a long passage so like the rest of his personal statements, so steeped in his individuality as we know it from his signed poems, so pathetic and so joyous, that it is hard to understand how the poem can be attributed to any one but Cynewulf. 'Few friends are left me now,' he says; 'they have fared away to their High Father. And I bide here, waiting till He on whose Rood I looked of old shall bring me to the happy place where the High God's folk are set at the evening meal.' And with that the poetry and the life of Cynewulf close.

The time is coming when his name will be more highly honoured among us, and his poetry better known. He had imagination; he anticipated, at a great distance, the Nature-poetry of the nineteenth century, especially the poetry of the sea; his personal poetry, full of religious passion both of penitence and joy, makes him a brother of the many poets who in England have written well of their own heart and of God in touch with it. His hymnic passages of exultant praise ought to be translated and loved by all who cherish the Divine praise which from generation to generation has been so nobly sung by English poets. The heroic passages in his poems link us to our bold heathen forefathers, and yet are written by a Christian. Their spirit is still the spirit of England. But his greatest hero was Jesus Christ. Cynewulf was, more than any other Old English poet, the man who celebrated Christ as the Healer of men, and, because He was the Healer, the Hero of the New Testament.

The other remains of English poetry which we possess in the *Exeter* and *Vercelli Books*, and which were written before the revival of literature under Ælfred, belong more to the history of criticism than literature. They were written at various dates during the eighth and ninth centuries. For our purpose it will almost suffice to name the best of them. One of them is a short *Physiologus*, a description of three animals—the Panther, the Whale, and the Partridge—followed by a religious allegory based on the description. The Panther symbolises Christ, the Whale the devil. There are two didactic poems, the *Address of a Father to a Son*, and *of the Lost Soul to its Body*. There are two other poems on the *Gifts of Men* and the

Fates of Men, the latter of which treats its subject with so much originality that it has been given to Cynewulf. Both contain passages which tell us a good deal about the arts and crafts of the English, and about various aspects of English scenery. The *Gnomic Verses*—folk proverbs and maxims, short descriptions of human life and of natural events—are in four collections, three in the *Exeter Book* and one in the *Cotton MS.* at Cambridge. Many of these are interesting. Some have come down from heathen times ; some are quotations from the poets ; others tell of war, of courts, of women, of games, of domestic life. They would have interested Ælfred ; and it is probable that, collected at York, they were edited in Wessex in Ælfred's time. The *Rune Song* is an alphabet of the Runes, with attached verses, such as we still make at the present day on the letters of the alphabet. There are two dialogues between *Solomon and Saturnus*, in which Christian wisdom in Solomon and the heathen wisdom of the East in Saturnus contend together in question and answer. Such dialogues became frequent in medieval literature, but changed their form. Marculf takes the place of Saturn, and represents the uneducated peasant or mechanic, whose rustic wit often gets the better of the king and the scholar. But there is no trace of this rebellion against Church and State in the English dialogues. With them we may close the poetry of the ninth century. A few years after the death of Cynewulf the Danish terror began. Literature decayed ; men had not the heart to write poetry ; and when, shortly after 867, the 'army' (which had already ravaged East Anglia and the greater part of Mercia) stormed York and destroyed every abbey and seat of learning from the Humber to the Forth, the poetry of Northumbria passed away. We may say that the farewell of Cynewulf in the *Dream of the Rood* was the dirge of Northumbrian song.

At the Judgment-Day.

Deep creation thunders, and before the Lord shall go
Hugest of upheaving fires o'er the far-spread earth !
Hurtles the hot flame, and the heavens burst asunder,
All the firm-set flashing planets fall out of their places.
Then the sun that erst o'er the elder world
With such brightness shone for the sons of men
Black-dark now becomes, changed to bloody hue.
And the moon alike, who to man of old
Nightly gave her light, nither tumbles down :
And the stars also shower down from heaven,
Headlong through the roaring lift, lashed by all the
    winds.

(From the Crist.)

The Bliss of Heaven.

There, is angels' song ; there, enjoyment of the blest ;
There, belovèd Presence of the Lord Eternal,
To the blessèd brighter than the beaming of the Sun !
There is love of the beloved, life without the end of
    death ;
Merry there man's multitude ; there unmarred is youth
    by eld ;
Glory of the hosts of Heaven, health that knows not
    pain ;
Rest for righteous doers, rest withouten strife,
For the good and blessed ! Without gloom the day,
Bright and full of blossoming ; bliss that 's sorrowless ;
Peace all friends between, ever without enmity ;
Love that envieth not, in the union of the saints,
For the happy ones of Heaven ! Hunger is not there
    nor thirst,
Sleep nor heavy sickness, nor the scorching of the Sun ;
Neither cold nor care ; but the happy company,
Sheenest of all hosts, shall enjoy for aye
Grace of God their King, glory with their Lord.

(From the Crist.)

St Guthlac dies and is received into Heaven.

          Then out-streamed a Light
Brightest that of beaming pillars ! All that Beacon fair,
All that heavenly glow round the holy home,
Was up-reared on high, even to the roof of Heaven,
From the field of earth, like a fiery tower,

Seen beneath the sky's expanse, sheenier than the sun,
Glory of the glorious stars ! Hosts of angels sang
Loud the lay of Victory ! In the lift the ringing sound
Now was heard the heaven under, raptures of the Holy
    Ones !
So the blessed Burgstead was with blisses filled,
With the sweetest scents, and with skiey wonders,
With the angels' singing, to its innermost recesses ;
Heirship of the Holy One !
                    More onelike it was,
And more winsome there, than in world of ours
Any speech may say ; how the sound and odour,
How the clang celestial, and the saintly song
Heard in Heaven were—high-triumphant praise of God,
Rapture following rapture.
                  All our island trembled,
All its Field-floor shook.

                  (From the *Guthlac.*)

Latin Writers before Ælfred.

When Augustine landed in Thanet in 597 and
made Canterbury the first Christian town, he
brought with him, to add to the development of
English literature, the power, the wisdom, the amal-
gamating force, and the long traditions of Rome.
But at first, though the Roman missionaries influenced the English thought, they did not use
the English language. All that they wrote they
wrote in Latin. The Celtic Church encouraged
the. English to shape their thought and feeling
in their own tongue ; the Roman Church dis-
couraged this ; and the south of England, where
Rome was supreme as a teacher, did not till the
days of Ælfred produce any important literature
in English.

The Latin literature of the south began with
Theodore of Tarsus, who was made Archbishop of
Canterbury in 669. Benedict Biscop, a Northumbrian scholar, came with him from Rome ; and
Benedict, going to his home, was the proper founder
of Latin literature in Northumbria. Hadrian, Theodore's deacon, joined in 671, and with his help

Theodore set on foot the school of Canterbury, which soon became the centre of southern learning. Wessex and Kent now produced their own scholars, and their bishops were men who loved and nourished education. Daniel of Winchester was a wise assistant of Bæda ; but the man who best represents the knowledge and literature of the south was Ealdhelm, who, educated by Mailduf, an Irishman, and also at Canterbury, became Abbot of Malmesbury and Bishop of Sherborne. He may have helped to compile the *Laws of Ine*, King of Wessex, and he made some English songs ; but his chief work was in Latin, and it was the Latin of a scholar who knew the Roman classics. He wrote Latin verse with ease, and translated into hexameters the stories of his prose treatise *De laudibus Virginitatis*. His Latin Riddles sent to Aldfrith of Northumbria were used by Cynewulf. His correspondence was extensive, and the letters to English and Welsh kings, to monasteries abroad, are as honourable to him as his letters to the abbesses and nuns, who in those days had learnt Latin, are charming, gay, and tender. His style is swollen, fantastic, and self-pleased, but the goodness and grace of the man shine through it. He was the last of the Wessex scholars who at this time did any literary work.

Ability and intelligence in Wessex were more employed in organisation of the Church and in missionary enterprise than in writing. Theodore brought the whole Christianity of England into unity. Winifried or Boniface, who brought Central Germany into obedience to the Roman See ; Willibald, one of our first pilgrims to Palestine ; Lullus, Archbishop of Mainz, who has left us a correspondence which proves his influence over the growth of Christianity and learning in England and Europe, were all West Saxons. But after the middle of the eighth century active literary life died in Wessex, and when Ælfred came to the throne in 871, there was not a single priest left who could understand their service books or put them into English.

The history of Latin literature in the Mid-England kingdom of Mercia is even of less importance than it is in Wessex. Under Æthelbald the country seems to have won a reputation for learning; and Ecgwin, Bishop of Worcester, is said to be our first autobiographer. The Life of St Guthlac, written by Felix of Crowland for an East Anglian king, in outpuffing Latin, is the only work we know of. But Æthelbald and his successor Offa were munificent to monasteries; and the school at Worcester was the last refuge of learning, when its cause was lost all over England in the ninth century.

The career of Latin literature in Northumbria was more continuous and more important than it was in Wessex or Mercia. The names of many of its scholars were known over the world, and are famous to this day. Northumbrian scholarship founded a great school, almost a university, at York, from which flowed the learning which, received and cherished by Charles the Great, produced an early Renaissance in Europe. The story of its rise and its fall belongs to York. The story of its growth and development belongs to Wearmouth and Jarrow.

Christianity reached York in the year 627, when Paullinus baptised Eadwine. But after Eadwine's death Northumbria relapsed into heathenism, Paullinus fled, and Latin literature was stifled in its birth. Literature and religion again took fresh life under Oswald in 634, but they were now in Celtic, not in Roman hands. The monasteries set up were ruled by Celtic monks from Iona; the bishops came from the same place; the kings and princes of the Northumbrian house were, for the most part, educated at Iona, spoke Irish, and knew the poetry and learning of Ireland. And the Irish, accustomed to praise God and their heroes and saints in their own tongue, encouraged the

Northumbrians to write in their own tongue. The first literature of Northumbria was in English.

Rome was naturally unsatisfied with this predominance of the Celtic Church ; Northumbria must be drawn into the Latin fold ; and Theodore, Wilfrid, and others, with Prince Alchfrith, fought their battle so well that in 664, at the Synod of Whitby, Northumbria joined the Latin Church. And now, though the Celtic influence lasted for many years, Latin learning, which had begun in Ripon and Hexham, took deep root in the north. Benedict Biscop, who had been at Rome with Theodore, built in 674 the monastery of St Peter at Wearmouth, and in 682 the sister house at Jarrow. He and the large libraries he collected for these abbeys were the real foundation of the Latin literature and learning of the north. Scholars and writers soon began to multiply. Wilfrid's biography—the first written in England —was done by his friend Eddius Stephanus about 709. The Life of St Cuthbert was written at Lindisfarne. Wilfrid's closest friend, Acca, Bishop of Hexham, increased the library which John of Beverley had ministered to. These are the chief names of the early Latin writers of the north.

But the learning was scattered. It was gathered together and generalised by **Bæda** of Jarrow. He is the master of the time, and his books became not only the sources of English, but of European learning. To this day his name is revered ; he is still called the ' Venerable Bede ; ' all the science, rhetoric, grammar, theology, and historical knowledge of the past which he could attain he absorbed, edited, and published. He increased in his *Homilies* and *Commentaries* the religious literature of the world ; he made delightful biographies, and he wrote the *Ecclesiastical History of the English Nation* with skill and charm. It is our best authority. His first books, on the scientific studies of the time, were written between 700 and 703. They were followed by a primer of the history of the world—*De sex ætatibus Sæculi*, 707 ; by the *Commentaries* on almost all the books of the Old and New Testaments, and these range over many years after 709 ; by the *Lives of Cuthbert and the Abbots of Wearmouth and Jarrow*, 716–20 ; and by the *De Temporum ratione* in 726. The *Ecclesiastical History* was finished in 731, and his last work, the *Letter to Egbert*, was done in the year of his death, 735. These thirty-five years were thus filled with that learning and teaching and writing in which he had always great delight ; and the little cell at Jarrow, whence he rarely stirred, was continually visited by men of many businesses and of all ranks in life. He kept in touch with all the monasteries of England, and with many in Europe. Even so far away as Rome he had scholars who worked for him among the archives. His greatest book is the *Ecclesiastical History*. He took so much pains to make it accurate, and to write nothing without consulting original and contemporary authorities, that the modern historical school claim him as their own. He shows in the book that power of choice and rejection of material so necessary for a historian ; and, what chiefly concerns us here, he filled it with a literary charm and beauty of statement when the subject permitted this self-indulgence. It is here that his personality most appears ; that we feel his happy, gentle, loving, and simple nature. His character adorns his style. The stories which embellish the book have a unique clearness and grace, a vivid grasp of character, a human tenderness, which makes us feel at times as if we were present with him in his room at Jarrow and listening to his charitable voice. Cuthbert, one of his pupils, gives an account of his fair death in his cell among his books ; and it is pleasant to think that the last work on which he was engaged on the day of his departure was a translation into English of the Gospel of St John, and that almost his last speech was the making of a few English verses, for, indeed, he was learned in English songs. (There is a translation from Bæda's *History* at page 53.)

The seat of learning at Bæda's death was transferred from Jarrow to York, where Ecgberht, Bæda's pupil, became an archbishop. The school he established at York may almost be termed a university. The education given was in all the branches of learning then known, in Ethica, Physica, and Logica. The library was the largest and the best outside of Rome, and was more useful than that at Rome. The arts were not neglected. The Latin Fathers ; the Roman poets, grammarians, orators ; the *Natural History* of Pliny, some of the Greek Fathers, and the Scriptures, were studied by a host of scholars from Ireland, Italy, Gaul, Germany, and England. When Ecgberht died Ælberht succeeded him, and with Alcuin's help increased the library and developed the education given in the schools. In 770 York and its library and schools was the centre of European learning. Ælberht's greatest friend was Alcuin (Eng. Ealhwine), the finest scholar York produced, and the last. His classical was as good as his patristic learning. His style has. earned him the name of the Erasmus of his century. He loved Virgil so well that pious persons, reproached him for it. His reputation came to the ears of Charles the Great, who was then starting the education of his kingdoms ; and Alcuin, who had met Charles at Pavia about 780, and again at Parma in 781, left England—though he revisited it in 790–92—to remain on the Continent till his death in the abbey of St Martin of Tours in 804. He left many books behind him—learned, theological, and virtuous. Of his Latin poems, that dedicated to the history of the great men of the school of York is the best. The *Letters*—more than three hundred—which he wrote to Charles and to most of the important personages in England and Europe, have the best right to the name of literature, and prove how wide was his influence, and how useful his work to the centuries that followed. He brought all the scholarship of England to the empire of the greatest man in Europe, whose power sent it far and wide. And he did this at the very time when its doom had begun to fall upon it in England. Alcuin himself heard of the ravaging of Lindisfarne by the Vikings in 793, and of the attack in the following year on Wearmouth, and cried out with pity and sorrow. The years that followed were years of decay. Northumbria was the prey of anarchy from 780 to 798. The six years of quiet that followed were years in which the school of York, weakened by Alcuin's absence, sickened and failed. In 827 Ecgberht of Wessex put an end to the separate kingdom of Northumbria. In 867 the Danish 'army' invaded the north, conquered York, settled there, and destroyed every abbey, both in Deira and Bernicia. Bishoprics, libraries, schools were all swept away. A little learning may have crept on in York, for the town was not destroyed, and it again flourished under Danish rule. Only one poor school of learning remained in that part of Mercia which was finally saved by Ælfred from the Danes. Worcester was the last refuge of the faded learning of Northumbria ; and when Ælfred began the revival of education in England, collected the old poetry, attempted to restore monastic leisure and scholarship, and himself, having learnt Latin, originated English prose by the translation of Latin books, it was from Worcester that he fetched the only Englishmen who could help him in his work.

Ælfred.

Ælfred, whose character was even greater than his renown as warrior, ruler, and lawgiver, was also a king in English literature. With him, at Winchester, began the prose-writing of England. His books were chiefly translations, but they were interspersed with original work which reveals to us his way of thinking, the temper of his soul, the interests of his searching intelligence, and his passion for teaching his people all that could then be known of England, of the history of the world, of religion, and of the Divine Nature. They appealed to the clergy, to the people, to scholars, to the warriors and sailors of England. Their aim was the education of his countrymen.

Born at Wantage in 849, he was the youngest son of Æthelwulf, and the grandson of the great Ecgberht. Rome, whither he went at the age of four years, and then again when he was six years old, made its deep impression on him. He stayed on his return at the court of Charles the Bald, and heard, no doubt, of the education which Charles the Great had given to the empire, for when he undertook a similar task in England he followed the methods and the practice of the emperor. When he arrived in England he sought for teachers, but found-none. When he was twenty years old he heard with indignant sorrow of the destruction of all learning in England by the Danes ; and the lover of learning as well as the patriot was whetted into wrath when, on the height of Ashdown, he and his brother Æthelred drove the Danes down the hill with a pitiless slaughter. Not long after this battle he became King of Wessex in 871. The work by which he made his kingdom belongs to history. It was only in 887 that he began his literary labour in a parenthesis of quiet. But he had made preparations for it beforehand. He had collected round him whatever scholars were left in England. They were few,—Werfrith, Bishop of Worcester ; Denewulf, of the same town ; Plegmund, Æthelstan, and Werwulf, all three from Mercia. With these he exhausted England. Then he sent to Flanders for Grimbald, whom he made Abbot of Winchester ; and to Corvëi in Westphalia for John the Old Saxon, whom he placed over his monastic house at Athelney. But his closest comrade in this work was Asser of St

David's, whom he induced to stay with him for six months in the year, who taught him Latin, and whose Latin Life of the king is, with all its inter-polations and errors, our best authority. The first thing they did together was Ælfred's *Hand-book*. When Asser quoted or Ælfred read out of the Bible or the Fathers any passage which interested the king, it was written down and translated into English in the note-book which the king kept in his breast. It was a book, then, of religious extracts, with here and there an illustration or a remark of Ælfred's added in his own words. This *Hand-book*, begun in November 887, was set forth for the use of the people in English in 888. The loss of it is a great misfortune.

The collection of the laws of Æthelberht, Ine, and Offa, with laws of his own, into a *Law-book* was the next work Ælfred undertook, and it was probably completed in 888. But the work of collection had most likely been begun in 885 or 886, for William of Malmesbury says that it was composed amid the noise of arms and the braying of the trumpets—that is, during the short struggle with the Danes in 885–86, when Ælfred secured London for his king-dom. The book was then in hand for more than two years. By this time he was acquainted with Latin, and as the clergy were the teachers of the people, the first book he translated was for their benefit. It was the *Cura Pastoralis*, the Herdsman's Book, of Gregory the Great, a manual of the duties of the clergy, the description of the ideal of a Christian priest ; and a copy was sent ' to every bishop's seat in my kingdom,' probably in the year 890. The book is the book of a beginner in translation. It is more close to its author than the other transla-tions. Several paragraphs in the Preface seem to speak of the work as the first translation he issued. No long original matter is inserted ; but the well-known *Preface* is from Ælfred's own hand, and it is the beginning of English prose literature. It breathes throughout of the king's character. It sketches the state of learning in England when he came to the throne, and we realise from it how much he did for literature, and the difficulties with which he had to contend. Its style is curiously simple and fresh, and it succeeds in its patriotic effort to be clear. It is plain here, as in his other writings, that Ælfred said to himself, 'I will try to make the most ignorant understand me.'

So many translations of this *Preface* have been published that it does not seem necessary to insert any quotation from it, but at the end Ælfred has added some verses of his own, and their simplicity, their faint imaginative note, their personal and tender religious feeling, their being perhaps the first verses that he wrote, induce me to paraphrase them :

These are the waters which the God of hosts promised for our comfort to us dwellers on the earth, and His will is that these ever-living waters should flow into all the world from all who truly believe in Him ; and their well-spring is the Holy Ghost. Some shut up this stream of wisdom in their mind so that it flows not everywhere in vain, but the well abides in the breast of the man, deep and still. Some let it run away in rills over the land, and it is not wise that such bright waters should, noisy and shallow, flow over the land till it becomes a fen. But now draw near to drink it, for Gregory has brought to your doors the well of the Lord. Whoever have brought a water-tight pitcher, let him fill it now, and let him come soon again. Whoever have a leaky pitcher, let him mend it, lest he spill the sheenest of waters and lose the drink of life.

The second book Ælfred translated was Bæda's *Ecclesiastical History of the English*, 890–91. It was done not only to instruct the clergy in the history of their Church, but also the people in the history of their own land. It omits several chapters of the original, and the king adds nothing of his own. We may wonder why he gave no particular account in it of the history of Church and State in Wessex, but this curious omission may be explained by the fact that in 891 he had begun to work up the *English Chronicle* into a national history, and did not care to write two accounts of the same matter.

A certain portion of the *Chronicle* already existed. This was probably made by Bishop Swithun of Winchester shortly after the death of Æthelwulf, and runs up to the year 855. It took the meagre annals made at Winchester as its basis, filled them from tradition back to Hengest, and then told at some length the wars and death of Æthelwulf. Ælfred, finding this account, caused it to be carefully investigated and written up to date, with a full history of his wars with the Danes. The style of this history is of the same kind throughout, and it is more than probable that it was the work of his own hand. Condensed, bold, rough, and accurate, it is a fine beginning of the historical prose of England. This is the manuscript of the Annals of Winchester, presented by Archbishop Parker to the library of Corpus Christi at Cambridge, and the copy is in one handwriting.

The next book the king translated, about 891–93, was the *History of the World* by Orosius. That history was written in 418 at the suggestion of St Augustine. It was the standard historical authority during the Middle Ages, and Ælfred edited it to teach his people all that was known of the world beyond England. He left out what he thought needless for them to know, and he filled it up from his own knowledge with matters of interest to Englishmen and with comments of his own. Among these was a full account of the geography of Germany, and of the countries where the English tongue had been spoken of old. To this he added the personal tales of two voyagers, Ohthere and Wulfstan, who had sailed along the coasts of Norway and the German shores of the Baltic. Ohthere had made two voyages, one northward as far as the mouth of the Dwina where it poured into the White Sea, the

other down the eastern coast of Denmark till
he saw the Baltic running upwards into the
land ; and the king adds, 'He had gone by the
lands where the Engle dwelt before they came
hither.' Wulfstan, starting from Haithaby, the
capital of the old Engle-land, went for seven days
and nights along the German coast till he reached
the Vistula. These journeys the king, sitting in
his chamber in the royal house, wrote down, probably from the dictation of the mariners. It is a
pleasant scene to look upon. The style of this
writing is, as usual, concise, simple, and straight-
forward, with a touch of personal pleasure in it.

These translations were the work of about five
years, from 888 to 893. In the latter year he was
interrupted by the invasion of the Viking Hasting
and the rising of the Danelaw. This was the
last effort of the Danes against him, and in 897
he had completely crushed it by the capture of
the Danish fleet. From that date till his death
in 901 he had the stillness he loved, and he
returned to his literary work. The book he now
undertook to translate (897–98) was the *De Consolatione Philosophiæ*, which Boethius had written
in prison to comfort his heart. It is a dialogue
between him and Philosophy, who consoles him
for trouble by proving that the only lasting happiness is in the soul. The wise and virtuous man
is master of all things. The book is the final
utterance of heathen Stoicism, but was so near
to the conclusions of Christianity that the Middle
Ages believed the writer to be a Christian ; and
his book was translated into the leading lan-
guages of Europe. Its serious, sorrowful, but
noble argument suited well with the circumstances
of Ælfred's life and with his spiritual character.
He added to Boethius long passages of his own ;
and the fifth book is nearly altogether rewritten by
the king. He filled the Stoic's thought with his
own profound Christianity, with solemn passages
on the Divine Nature and its relation to man's will

and fate, with aspiring hopes and prayers. Many inserted paragraphs have to do with his own life, with the government of his kingdom, with his thoughts and feelings as a king, with his scorn of wealth and fame and power in comparison with goodness. He stands in its pages before us, a noble figure, troubled, but conqueror of his trouble ; master of himself ; a lover of God and his people, dying, but with a certain hope of immortal peace.

Whether he or another translated into English verse the *Metra* with which Boethius interspersed his prose is not as yet settled by the critics. If we believe the short poetical prologue to the oldest of the manuscripts, the English version of the *Metra* in poetry is the work of the king, and it would illustrate his intellectual activity if we could be sure he translated them into verse. But we do not know. Nor do we know for certain what else he did before his death. It is more or less agreed that he made a translation which we possess of the *Soliloquia* of St Augustine, and the Preface to this book by the writer is a pathetic farewell to his work as a translator, and a call to others to follow his example for the sake of England. Its parabolic form makes it especially interesting. A letter of St Augustine's, *De Videndo Deo*, is added to the Dialogue between St Augustine and his Reason. The English translation of the whole is divided into three dialogues, and the first two are called a 'Collection of Flowers.' The third dialogue closes with 'Here end the sayings of King Ælfred,' and the date is probably 900.

His last work—and it fits his dying hand—was a translation of the Psalms of David. It is supposed, but very doubtfully, that we have in the first fifty psalms of the *Paris Psalter* this work of Ælfred's. He did not live to finish it. In 901 this noble king, the 'Truth-teller,' 'England's Darling,' 'the unshakable pillar of the West Saxons, full of justice, bold in arms, and filled with the knowledge that flows from God,' passed away, and was laid to rest at Winchester.

Only two books not done by himself were, as far as we know, set forth in his reign. One was the *Dialogues of Gregory*, translated, by Ælfred's request, by Werfrith, Bishop of Worcester. Ælfred wrote the Preface, and it breathes throughout of his kingly character. The other was the *Book of Martyrs*, a year's calendar of those who had witnessed to the Faith. It does not follow that no other books but these were written during his reign in English, but it is probable that Ælfred stood almost alone as an English writer. Asser's Life of the king was in Latin. On the whole Ælfred's efforts to make a literary class, even the schools he established for that purpose, were a failure. It was not till nearly a hundred years after him that the work he did for English bore fruit in the revival of English prose by Ælfric.

Ælfred was not a literary artist, but he had the spirit of a scholar. His desire for knowledge was insatiable. His love of the best was impassioned. It is a pity Asser did not bring him into contact with Virgil and the rest of the great Romans. But England had the first claim on him, and he collected with eagerness the English poems and songs. He translated from Bæda his country's history ; he himself shaped a national history ; he collected and arranged the English laws of his predecessors, and he added new laws of his own and his Witan's. He taught his people the history of other lands. He had as great an eagerness to teach as to learn. He was not only the warrior, the law-giver, the ruler, but the minister of education. And the style in which he did his work, reveals the simple, gracious, humble, loving character of the man. It is steeped in his natural personality, and it charms through that more than through any literary ability. It is always clear ; its aim is to be useful to his people ; and it gains a certain weight and dignity from his long experience in public affairs, in war and policy. The impression he has made on England is indelible, and his spirit has not ceased to move among us.

Ælfred and the Work of a King.

Reason ! indeed thou knowest that neither greed nor the power of this earthly kingdom was ever very pleasing to me, neither yearned I at all exceedingly after this earthly kingdom. But yet indeed I wished for material for the work which it was bidden me to do, so that I might guide and order with honour and fitness the power with which I was trusted. Indeed thou knowest that no man can show forth any craft ; can order, or guide any power, without tools or material—material, that is, for each craft, without which a man cannot work at that craft. This is then the material of a king and his tools, wherewith to rule—That he have his land fully manned, that he have prayer-men, and army-men, and workmen. Indeed thou knowest that without these tools no king can show forth his craft. This also is his material—That he have, with the tools, means of living for the three classes—land to dwell upon, and gifts, and weapons, and meat, and ale, and clothes, and what else the three classes need.

And this is the reason I wished for material wherewith to order (my) power, in order that my skill and power should not be forgotten and hidden away, for every work and every power shall soon grow very old and be passed over silently, if it be without wisdom ; because whatsoever is done through foolishness no one can ever call work. Now would I say briefly that I have wished to live worthily while I lived, and after my life to leave to men who should come after me my memory in good deeds.

(From the *De Consolatione Philosophiæ*.)

Ælfred's Preface to the 'De Consolatione.'

King Ælfred was the translator of this book, and turned it from Latin into English as it is now done. Sometimes he set down word for word, sometimes meaning for meaning, as he could translate most plainly and clearly in spite of the various and manifold worldly cares which often occupied him in mind and body. These cares, which in his days came on the kingship he had undertaken, are very hard for us to number. And yet, when he had learned this book and turned it from Latin into the English tongue, he then wrought it afterwards into verse, as it is now done. And now he begs, and for God's sake prays every one whom it may please to read the book, that he pray for him, and that he blame him not if he understood it more rightly than he (the king) could. For every one, according to the measure of his understanding and leisure, must speak what he speaketh and do what he doeth.

Ælfred's Prayer.

Lord God Almighty, shaper and ruler of all creatures, I pray Thee for Thy great mercy, and for the token of the holy rood, and for the maidenhood of St Mary, and for the obedience of St Michael, and for all the love of Thy holy saints and their worthiness, that Thou guide me better than I have done towards Thee. And guide me to Thy will to the need of my soul better than I can myself. And stedfast my mind towards Thy will and to my soul's need. And strengthen me against the temptations of the devil, and put far from me foul lust and every unrighteousness. And shield me against my foes, seen and unseen. And teach me to do Thy will, that I may inwardly love Thee before all things with a clean mind and clean body. For Thou art my maker and my redeemer, my help, my comfort, my trust, and my hope. Praise and glory be to Thee now, ever and ever, world without end. Amen.

(*De Cons.*, Bk. v.)

Poetry from Ælfred to the Conquest.

During the reign of Ælfred poetry was not altogether neglected in Wessex. It is more than probable that it was at the king's instance that the poetry of Northumbria was collected and translated into the dialect of Wessex, in which dialect we now possess it. Among the rest we may surely count the lost poems of Cædmon of which Ælfred had read when he translated the *Ecclesiastical History*. Then also, *Genesis A*, whether by Cædmon or not, now appeared in West Saxon. Now, there was a great gap in the manuscript after the line 234, and some copyist of the poem inserted, in order, to fill up the space, lines 235–851, out of an Old Saxon poem (it is supposed) which had been translated into West Saxon. It is thought from certain similarities in diction, manner, and rhythm that this Old Saxon poem (some lines of which, identical with corresponding lines in the West Saxon insertion, have been lately discovered) was written by the writer of the *Heliand* or by some imitator of his in Old Saxony. At any rate this poem was brought to England, translated, and a portion of it, relating to the Fall of Man, was used to fill up the gap in *Genesis A*. We call this portion *Genesis B*, and it differs from the earlier *Genesis* not only in manner, metre, and language, but in sentiment and thought.

It opens with the fall of the rebel angels already told in *Genesis A*. Lucifer, 'beauteous in body, mighty of mind,' seems to himself to be equal with God, and his pride is injured by the creation of man. And the fierce soliloquy into which his insolent Teutonic individuality outbreaks is one of the finest passages in Anglo-Saxon poetry. He is flung into hell, and hafted down by bars across his neck and breast in the centre of that abyss of pain—swart, deep-valleyed, swept at morn by north-east wind and frost, and then by leaping flame and bitter smoke. 'Oh, how unlike,' he cries, 'this narrow stead to that home in heaven's high kingdom which of old I knew! Adam holds my seat; this is my greatest sorrow! But could I break forth for one short winter hour with all my host—but God knew my heart, and forged these gratings of hard steel, else an evil work would be between man and me. Oh, shall we not have vengeance! Help me, my thanes; fly to earth; make Adam and Eve break God's bidding; bring them down to hell; then I shall softly rest in my chains.' One of his thanes springs up, and beating the fire aside, finds Adam at last and Eve standing beside the two trees in Eden. The temptation

follows, and it is subtly borne. Adam rejects it ;
Eve yields, and after a whole day persuades
Adam to eat the fruit. Then the scornful fiend
breaks into a wild cry of satisfied vengeance.
' My heart is enlarged. I have never bowed the
knee to God. O Thou, my Lord, who liest in
sorrow, rejoice now, laugh, and be blithe; our
harms are well avenged.'

Adam and Eve are left conscious of their fall.
Their love is not shattered ; there is no mutual
reproach. Eve's tenderness is as deep as Adam's
repentance, and they fall to prayer. This is the
close of *Genesis B.* It is full of Teutonic feeling.
The fierce individuality ; the indignant pride ; the
fury for vengeance, the joy of its accomplishment ;
the close comradeship between the lord and his
thanes ; the tenderness and devotion of the
woman ; the reverence of the man for the woman ;
the intensity of the repentance—may all be
matched from the Icelandic sagas, and they prove
that the spirit which afterwards made those sagas
was alive in England in the ninth and tenth
centuries.

The second part of the poems which pass under
the name of Cædmon, and which had the name of
Christ and Satan, are now allotted by the majority
of critics to the tenth century, and, presumably,
to Wessex. Their simple, direct, and passionate
elements, their imaginative grasp of their subjects,
seem more Northumbrian than West Saxon, and
this is not an impossible opinion. They are now
divided into three poems or fragments of poems,
the first of which is called the *Fallen Angels*, the
second the *Harrowing of Hell*, and the third the
Temptation. The character of Satan in them
differs greatly from that in *Genesis A* or *B*, and
so does the description of hell. The bond of
comradeship between his thanes and Satan has
perished, but not that between Christ and His
thanes. Satan, in an agony of longing for heaven,
repents, but no mercy is given to him. Dialogue

enlivens the poems, and their exultant bursts of
religious praise recall the spirit of Cynewulf. The
personages are drawn with much humanity. The
descriptions are vivid and imaginative. We see
Satan wandering and wailing in his misty hall,
the weltering sea of fire outside, the cliffs and
burning marl of hell, the fiends flying before
Christ when He comes to break down the gates.
We watch the good spirits in Hades lifting
themselves, leaning on their hands when He came ;
their ascent with Him to the feast in the heavenly
burg, and the fall of Satan from the Mount of
Temptation through a hundred thousand miles to
the abyss of hell.

These are the last religious poems before the
Conquest which show any traces of imaginative or
original power. The rest of which we know seem
to be the dry and lifeless productions of monks in
the cloisters, and are nothing better than alliterative
prose. There are a crowd of versions of the Creed,
the Lord's Prayer, and the Canticles. The *Last
Judgment*, a poem from which Wulfstan quotes in
a homily of 1010 ; a saints' calendar entitled the
Menologium, a metrical translation of fifty psalms,
scattered through a service book ; the translation
of the *Metra* of Boethius, if Ælfred did not do it ; a
poem advising a gray-haired warrior to a Christian
life, and another urging its readers to prayer,
almost exhaust the religious poetry of the tenth
and eleventh centuries before the Conquest. With
the exception of a few lines describing in the
Menologium the coming of summer, they are
totally devoid of any literary value. Religious
poetry had died.

But this was not the case with secular poetry.
Ballads and war-songs on any striking story of the
lives of kings or chiefs, dirges at their deaths, were
made all over England. The old sagas were put
into new forms ; the country families and the
villages had their traditionary songs. None of
these are left with the exception of the *Battle*

of Brunanburh and the *Battle of Maldon*, and a few fragments inserted in the *Chronicle*. A few prose records, also, in the *Chronicle* are supposed to be taken from songs current at the time. Moreover, it is plain from the statements of Henry of Huntingdon and William of Malmesbury that they used ballads of this time in their histories. Moreover, the old sagas were sung by wandering minstrels at every village fair, in the halls of the burgs, in the tents and round the bivouacs of the soldiers ; and the chieftain's bard, after every deed of war, sang the doings and the deaths of the warriors when the feast was set at night. There may have been other poems of a more thoughtful character, like the *Rhyme-Poem* in the *Exeter Book*, which belongs to the tenth century. It is the only poem in the English tongue which is written in the Scandinavian form called *Runhenda*, in which the last word of the first half of the verse is rhymed, in addition to the usual alliteration, with the last word of the second half. This form was used by Egill Skallagrimsson, the Icelandic skald, in the poem by which he saved his life from Erik Blood-Axe in 938. Egill was twice in England, and was a favourite of King Æthelstan. It is supposed that he made known this form of poetry to the writer of the *Rhyme-Song*, and this supposition is the origin of the date assigned to it—940–50. It is worth little in itself, and its subject is one common to English song—the contrast between a rich and joyous past and a wretched present.

It is pleasant to turn from it to the noble songs of **Brunanburh** and Maldon. At Brunanburh, in the year 937, England, under Æthelstan, Ælfred's grandson, vindicated her short-lived unity against the Danes, the Welsh, and the Scots, under Anlaf the Dane and Constantinus the king of the Scots. The song, recast by Tennyson, is no unworthy beginning of the war-poetry of England. Its patriotism is as haughty as that of the 'Fight at Agincourt,' the 'Battle of the Baltic,' and the 'Charge of the Light Brigade.' It resembles them, also, in its rough and clanging lines, in its singing and abrupt stanzas. Its English style is excellent, and it has the old heathen ring. It gives us a high idea of the value of the lost battle-songs of Old England.

The **Fight at Maldon** is of a different character. It is not so much of a composition. It reads as if it were written by an eyewitness. It uses the heroic terms; the warriors challenge one another as they do in the sagas, as they have done since the days of Homer. The tie that knitted chief to thane and thane to chief is as keenly dwelt on as it is in *Genesis* and in *Beowulf*. The rude cries of defiance are like those in the *Fight at Finnsburg*. The charge of cowardice, of faithlessness to their oath of service, which is made against those who flee the fight might have been written by one who had read the similar passage in *Beowulf*. The boasting and praise of those who died defending their lord might also be drawn from *Beowulf*. It is clear that this poem, written at the end of the tenth century—in 991—is as frankly heroic as any heathen poem. The old spirit lived on in the songs of war.

The battle is fought on the east of England, in the estuary of an Essex river. A roving Viking band, sailing up the river Panta, land on the spit of ground that divides the stream into two branches. On the northern shore lay Maldon, and Earl Byrhtnoth comes to do battle with the pirates. The tide is full, and for a long time the ford is impassable. The two bands shoot at one another with arrows. At last the ebb allowed them to meet at the ford and on the bank, where Byrhtnoth, in his chivalry, permitted them to land. But the Danes were too many for the English, and the great Earl died on the field. And his thanes, save a few cowards, died round him, fighting to the last.

His death-song is not like that of Beowulf. For the first time in English battle-poetry the chieftain dies with a Christian cry upon his lips. It is the beginning of a new element in the poetry of war. He dies as the knights die in the *Chansons de Geste*. Their last words are a prayer to Christ. We seem to feel in this change the breath of a new life, of a new world —of the life and world of romance. After this poem silence follows. The *Fight at Maldon* is the last song of the war-poetry of England before the Conquest. Not till long after the Conquest did it rise again, and then it rose almost a stranger to the ancient English ways. The Celtic and the Norman spirit had transformed it ; but deep below, and lasting through centuries of English song, the strong, constant, deep-rooted elements of the Teutonic race lay at the foundation of the English poetry of physical and moral battle.

Eve, after she has eaten of the Tree of Knowledge.

Sheener to her seemed all the sky and earth ;
All this world was lovelier ; and the work of God,
Mickle was and mighty then, though 'twas not by man's device,
That she saw (the sight)—but the Scather eagerly
Moved about her mind.
'Now thyself thou mayest see, and I need not speak it—
O thou, Eve the good, how unlike to thy old self
Is thy beauty and thy breast since thou hast believed my words.
    Light is beaming 'fore thee now,
Glittering against thee, which from God I brought,
White from out the Heavens. See thy hands may touch it !
Say to Adam then, what a sight thou hast,
And what powers—through my coming !'

Then to Adam wended Eve, sheenest of all women,
Winsomest of wives, e'er should wend into the world,
For she was the handiwork of the heavenly King.
                  Of the fruit unblest
Part was hid upon her heart, part in hand she bore.
'Adam, O my Lord, this apple is so sweet,
Blithe within the breast; bright this messenger;
'Tis an Angel good from God! By his gear I see
That he is the errand-bringer of our heavenly King!
             I can see Him now from hence
Where Himself He sitteth, in the south-east throned,
All enwreathed with weal; He who wrought the world.
And with Him I watch His angels, wheeling round about
    Him,
In their feathered vesture, of all folks the mightiest,
Winsomest of war-hosts! Who could wit like this
Give me, did not God Himself surely grant it me?
. . . . . . Far away I hear—
And as widely see—over all the world,
O'er the universe widespread!—All the music mirth
In the Heavens I can hear!—In my heart I am so clear,
Inwardly and outwardly, since the apple I have tasted.
See! I have it here, in my hands; O my good Lord!
Gladly do I give it thee; I believe from God it comes!'

Repentance of Adam and Eve.

' Thou mayst it reproach me, Adam, my beloved,
In these words of thine; yet it may not worse repent
    thee,
Rue thee in thy mind, than it rueth me in heart.'
Then to her for answer Adam spoke again—
'O if I could know the All-Wielder's will,
What I for my chastisement must receive from Him,
Thou should'st never see, then, anything more swift,—
    though the sea within
Bade me wade the God of Heaven, bade me wend me
    hence
In the flood to fare—Nor so fearfully profound
Nor so mighty were the Ocean, that my mind should
    ever waver—
Into the abyss I'd plunge, if I only might
Work the will of God!'

                        (From *Genesis B.*)

Prose from Ælfred to the Conquest.

Ælfred, though he began the prose of England, failed in establishing it. No results, save one, followed his work till ninety years had passed away. The one exception was the narrative in the *Chronicle* of the wars and government of Eadweard, Ælfred's son, 910–924. Ælfred's own work on the *Chronicle* ceased in 891. Another writer of vigour, earnestness, and conciseness told the story of the years from 894 to 897. From 897 to 910 the record is meagre, but a new life was given to the *Chronicle* by the narrative which began with 910. It may have been written by the same man who wrote of the years 894–97. His work ceases with the death of Eadweard, and it is the sole piece of secular prose which we possess at this date. From 925 to 940, during the reign of Æthelstan, the shallow records of the *Chronicle* are only once filled by the *Song of Brunanburh* (see page 24). From 940 to 975, during the reigns of Eadmund, Eadred, and Eadgar, the *Chronicle* contains nothing but short annual statements of leading events. Three small poems are inserted in it.

Secular prose then had died at Winchester. But religious prose now began to rise again with the revival of monasticism, begun by Dunstan and nursed into life by King Eadgar. Dunstan, in whom Celtic and English elements mingle, set up a school at Glastonbury, and made his pupils love the arts of music, of poetry, of design and embroidery, of gold-working, painting, and engraving, in all of which he was himself a master. He sang the Psalms with his boys, developed church ritual and music, drew the Irish scholars to his help, made a fine library and treasury, and, having trained his monks in all the known branches of learning, sent them forth as missionaries of education to various parts of England. His best scholar, Æthelwold, was made head of the Abbey of Abingdon, refounded by King Eadred; and Æthelwold, who died in 904, soon made Abingdon as good a school as Glastonbury. It was his favourite pupil, Ælfric, who created the new prose of England.

This revival of English prose kept step with the revival of monasticism. Monasticism had fallen into complete decay when Eadgar came to the throne in 959. Dunstan's effort, assisted as he was by Oswald of Ramsey and Odo of Canterbury, had not pushed it far. Even the *Rule* itself of Benedict had slipped out of memory, and Oswald and Æthelwold had to go or send to Fleury to recover it. But Eadgar threw himself eagerly into the movement, and Æthelwold, now Bishop of Winchester in 963, gave his full energy to the work. He cleared Winchester of the lazy secular clergy; he refounded Ely, Peterborough, and Thorney. No better work could be done for literature than this re-creation of the monasteries. Art, the science of medicine, the study of the Scriptures, of philosophy, of astronomy, and of literature, revived with their revival. The preaching and homilies of the monks brought religion as well as a kind of education to the people. And the new teaching was now given in the language of the people. At last the work of Ælfred began to produce its fruit.

Æthelwold loved his native tongue; King Ælfred's books were studied at Abingdon, and his principle—Teach Englishmen in English—was followed and established. The *Blickling Homilies*, nineteen of which exist, and probably the *Homilies* in the *Vercelli Book* belong to the early time of the monastic revival—from 960 to 990. They represent, with certain books mentioned by Ælfric and now lost, the transition between the prose of Ælfred and that of Ælfric.

A new and more literary English prose now began with **Ælfric.** He was born about 955, and educated at Winchester. Ælfhead, Æthelwold's successor, sent him in 987 to teach and govern the new monastery of Cerne Abbas in Dorset-shire, and here he first followed King Ælfred's plan, and translated Latin books into English for the use of the people. He returned to Win-chester in 989, where he continued his work till the Thane Æthelmær, who had founded a Benedictine monastery at Eynsham, near Oxford, made him its abbot. There, in that quiet place, he lived, learning and teaching, until he died about 1022.

His first book, *Homiliæ Catholicæ*, 990–94, is dedicated to Archbishop Sigeric, and consists of two collections of homilies, forty in each collection, on the Sundays and feast-days of the year. A small number of them are in alliterative verse. Then he composed the *Grammar* and the *Glossary*, which were probably followed by the *Colloquium*. As the Homilies addressed the people, these books addressed the pupils at the school of Winchester. The *Colloquium* is a discourse on the occupations of the monks and on various states of life ; and as one of the manuscripts has an English transla-tion over its lines, it becomes a kind of vocabulary. It was re-done by another Ælfric, one of his scholars, Ælfric Bata, with appendices. The lives of the saints, *Passiones Sanctorum*, another set of homilies, followed in 996. Other works of less importance were now taken up ; but, urged thereto by Thane Æthelweard, he began to translate the Bible, part of which, from Genesis xxiv. to the end of Leviticus, Æthelweard had given to another hand. The beginning, then, of Genesis was done by Ælfric, with Numbers, Deuteronomy, Joshua, Judges, Esther, Job, and Judith. The books are not literally translated ; parts are omitted, and parts are thrown into homiletic form. Ælfric used the same liberties with the Bible which Ælfred had used with Boethius and Orosius ; and he gave this work the same patriotic tinge as Ælfred had given to his translation of Orosius. The heroic sketches he made out of the Bible of the warriors of Israel not only taught the people the sacred history, but were also applied by him to encourage Englishmen against their foes. 'I have set forth *Judith*,' he says, 'in English for an example to you men that ye may guard your country against her foes ;' and he closes the Homilies with a hymn of praise to God for the great men in all history who had borne witness to the faith, and among them to Ælfred, Æthelstan, and Eadgar, the noble champions of England.

The *Canones Ælfrici*, which followed his translations of the Bible, were written about the year 1000. They were in Latin and addressed to the clergy. In 1006 or 1007, when he was Abbot of Eynsham, he made a book of extracts from the writings of his master, Æthelwold—*De Consuetudine Monachorum*; addressed a homily on forgiveness to his friend Wulfgeat, a royal thane at Ilmington ; another on chastity to Thane Sigeferth ; and about the same time, 1008, composed a treatise *Concerning the Old and New Testament*, which was a practical introduction to the study of the Scriptures. Then, turning from English to Latin prose, he wrote a sympathetic life of his master, *Vita Æthelwoldi*, and a *Sermo ad Sacerdotes* for Wulfstan, Bishop of Worcester, about 1014–16 ; and Wulfstan made him turn it into English. Other homilies, needless to record, he also made, and then died quietly between 1020 and 1025.

Ælfric was the Bæda of his time. He was the assimilator, collector, and distributor of learning, not its creator. He had no originality, but he loved his work and his country. The principles of education which Ælfred had established he carried out steadily. He trained the people as well as the clergy in their duties, in the history of the Church abroad and at home ; and his charming character, full of moral dignity, tact, gentle charity, and wisdom in affairs, recommended and enhanced his books and letters. In one thing he was original—in his style. He made a new, a lighter, more musical, more lissome prose. He fitted English to take up the number of new subjects which were soon to engage the interests of the country. We cannot tell what English prose might have become had this modern style been developed. But the Danish invasion checked and the Norman Conquest paralysed it for a long time. Ælfric's English prose had, however, one great fault. It became more and more alliterative—that is, it was prose written in poetic form. This manner, chiefly practised in his *Homilies*, may have been used to please the people and for their sake, but it injures the life of prose, and, when continued, kills it.

The creation of this new, popular, and flexible prose was one result of Ælfric's work. Another result was the increase of learning and of a higher life among the clergy. The Archbishops Sigeric and Wulfstan, the Bishops Wulfsige and Kenulf, were inspired by him, and they begged him to write such books in English as would enable them to teach their clergy the rudiments of learning and the practice of a holy life. And the effort was not in vain. The clergy began to have a higher ideal of their profession, and to follow it ; and so many small books on various ecclesiastical and theological matters were put forward in the eleventh century that it is plain the English clergy at the Conquest were not so ignorant as the Normans declared them to be.

A third result of Ælfric's work was the creation of a small literary class among the nobles, some of whom now became learners and patrons of literature. Æthelweard, probably the writer of the Chronicle which bears his name, a royal thane, urged Ælfric to write and began his translation of the Bible. Æthelmær, his son, was Ælfric's close friend and patron, and brought him into friendship with Wulfgeat, Sigweard, and Sigeferth, also nobles, for whom he wrote books. It is clear that the class Ælfred was unable to touch had now begun to be a cultivated class.

The mass of the people were also educated by the great body of homilies which Ælfric had written for them ; and the legends of the saints and the tales of the martyrs, going hand-in-hand with the saga stories over England, awakened the imagination of the farmer and the peasant.

Then, too, the monasteries, under his influence, now became the home of learned men who wrote on science as well as on theology. Byrchtfercth, of the monastery at Ramsey, was a well-known mathematician ; and his commentaries on the scientific works of Bæda, and his Life of Dunstan, prove his literary activity. The varied knowledge shown in these books, which date before 1016, makes it almost certain that he was the writer of a *Hand-book* in English which discusses the alphabets and subjects belonging to natural philosophy. Then a number of medical books were published in this eleventh century. The *Læce-Boc* of the tenth century was re-edited, with many interesting additions ; the *Herbarium Apuleii*, the *Medicina de Quadrupedibus*, and others of the same kind show how active were the dispensaries of the monasteries. Many religious books — translations of the Psalms, the Gospels, and the Pseudo-gospels, Biographies of the Fathers, of the martyrs, of saints, and a number of sermons — belong also to the first half of the eleventh century. Certain books of a proverbial and ethical tendency — a Dialogue between *Salomo and Saturnus*, another between the Emperor *Adrianus and Ritheus*, a selection from the *Disticha* of Cato — illustrate that English love for sententious literature which had arisen long before Ælfred, and which was afterwards, in the *Proverbs of Ælfred*, connected with his name. The *Glossaries*, in which the Latin is explained by English words, show how much Ælfric had brought Latin into English learning. The *Ritual of Durham* now added to itself a Northumbrian gloss. The splendid *Evangelium of Lindisfarne* was now interlineated, and so were the Rushworth Gospels.

There was, then, no little literary activity in the first half of this century. But it would have been much greater had not England again been fighting for her life with the Danes. In 1010 Thurkill began those dreadful raids in which East Anglia, Oxfordshire, Buckingham, Bedford, Northampton, Wiltshire, and other parts of Wessex were ravaged and plundered, and Ælfhead, Archbishop of Canterbury, was murdered in his burning town. Wulfstan, Archbishop of York 1002–23, heard of these horrors, and his *Sermo Lupi* (he called himself Lupus) *ad Anglos quando Dani maxime persecuti sunt eos*, in which he tells the tale of the invasion, and blames the sins and cowardice of the English, places him among the prose-writers of England. Some other homilies he wrote, but the passion and indignation with which he filled this sermon, and its weighty and vigorous English, isolate it from the rest. He sits closest to Ælfric, who saw along with him the outbreak of the Danish storm.

During the Danish rule over England no fresh literature was produced, but the coming of the Normans with Edward the Confessor not only strengthened the tendency, which had begun under Ælfric, to write in Latin rather than in English, but also introduced, and for the first time into English, tales from the East already tinged with the thoughts, feelings, colour, and life which were to grow into the full body of medieval Romance. The history of *Apollonius of Tyre*, used by Shakespeare in the play of *Pericles*, was now rendered into English prose out of the Latin translation of the late Greek story. Two other translations out of the Latin reproductions of the Greek legends of the life of Alexander—the *Letters of Alexander to Aristotle from India* and the *Wonders of the East* —were also made, and brought with them the air and the scenery of a new world. They are put into excellent English—the last fine English of the times before the Conquest, the last fruit, with the exception of the *Chronicle*, of the tree which Ælfred had planted ; and which, when it grew again above the soil, bore so changed an aspect that its original planters would not have recognised it. Its roots were the same ; its branches and foliage were different. Ælfred would have been puzzled to read the English in which the *Ancren Riwle* (the Rule of Anchoresses) was written in the reign of Henry III. It was the first Middle English Prose.

The English of the *Chronicle* illustrates this transition. The *Chronicle* is the continuous record of English history in English prose, and it passes undisturbed through the Norman Conquest up to the death of Stephen. Its *Winchester Annals* practically cease in 1005, or even earlier. They were preserved in Canterbury from 1005 to 1070, but there are only eleven entries during these sixty-five years, and these were made after the Conquest, at the election of Lanfranc as archbishop. The rest of these Annals is written in Latin, and they end with the consecration of Anselm. What Winchester dropped Worcester continued. The *Worcester Annals* were carefully kept to the year 1079. If they were continued to 1107, that continuation was merged in the *Annals of Peterborough.* The *Worcester Annals* of the *Chronicle* are written in the English of Ælfric, and were probably done by Bishop Wulfstan, who held the see from 1062 to 1095, and by Colman, his chaplain, who wrote the bishop's life in English.

The *Peterborough Annals* were only fully edited after the rebuilding of the monastery in 1121. This fine and full edition of the *Chronicle* was made up out of the Annals of Winchester, Worcester, and Abingdon, and was then continued probably by one hand to the year 1131. Another hand, using a more modern English, carried it on from 1132 to 1154, when it closed with the accession of Henry II. The records at Worcester and Peterborough are not unworthy of the first records at

Winchester. The Wars of Harold and the Fight at Stamford Bridge are boldly and picturesquely written. Even more picturesque is the account another writer gives of Senlac, and of William's stark, cruel, and just rule. This writer had lived at William's court, and we trace in his finer historical form that he had studied the Norman historians. The Peterborough scribe who followed him is rather a romantic than a national historian, and loves his monastery more than his nation. The second scribe of Peterborough, who probably composed his work in 1150–54, is well-known for his pitiful and patriotic account of the miseries of England under the oppression of the Norman nobles. When in 1154 the *Chronicle* was closed, the Norman chroniclers took up the history of England and wrote it in Latin ; but the *English Chronicle* remains for English literature the most ancient and venerable monument of English prose.

After the Conquest.

The Norman Conquest put an end to Old English literature. When that literature arose again its language and its spirit were transformed. Old English had become Middle English. Its prose, which was religious, had been profoundly changed by the Norman theology and the Norman enthusiasm for a religious life. Its poetry, equally touched by the Anglo-Norman religion and love of romance, adopted as its own the romantic tales, melodies, manners, and ways of thinking which came to it from France, both in religious and in story-telling poetry. But this change took nearly a century and a half before it began to bear fruit. During those long years of transition little English work was done, and none of it could be called literature. Old English writings, such as the *Homilies* of Ælfric and the *Translations of the Gospels* made in the eleventh century, and now called the *Hatton Gospels*, were copied and modernised. Monasteries, remote from Norman interests, still clung to, and made their little manuals and service books in, the English tongue. English prose was just kept alive, but only like a man in catalepsy.

English poetry had a livelier existence ; but we have no remains of the songs which were sung throughout the country, and which kept alive in the soul of franklin, peasant, and outlaw the glories and heroes of the past. We know that these were made and sung from the Norman chroniclers who used them, and from suggestions of them in the *Brut* of Layamon. Lays were made after the Conquest of the great deeds of Hereward, and are used in the Latin life of that partisan. Even in the twelfth century, songs were built on the old sagas, such as those which celebrated Weland and Wade, his father ; and sagas like *Horn, Havelok, Bevis of Hampton, Guy of Warwick*, and *Waltheof*, which took original form in English in the thirteenth century, existed as popular lays in the eleventh and twelfth. The noble figure of Ælfred appears again in the poem entitled the *Proverbs of Ælfred*, an ethical poem of sententious sayings, varying forms of which arose in the twelfth century.

Old English poetry, having neither rhyme nor a fixed number of syllables, depended on accent and alliteration. Every verse was divided into two half-verses by a pause, and had four accented syllables, the number of unaccented syllables being indifferent ; and the two half-verses were linked together by alliteration. The two accented syllables of the first half and one of the accented syllables of the second half began with the same consonant, or with vowels which were generally different from one another. But often there was only one alliterative letter in the first half-verse ; and the metre was further varied by the addition of unaccented syllables. The lays made after the Conquest illustrate the transition from the old alliterative metre to the short line and rhyme which were soon established by the Anglo-Normans when they began to write in English. The *Poema Morale* is thought by some to have first taken shape early in the twelfth century. In that case, it and other twelfth-century poems of little account bring us still nearer to Middle English poetry, if they do not form part of it ; but it is best, when we speak of literature, to make Middle English poetry properly begin with the first noble piece of poetic literature, with the *Brut* of Layamon, at the beginning of the thirteenth century.

STOPFORD A. BROOKE.

BIBLIOGRAPHY.—The MS. of *Beowulf* is in the Cottonian Library in the British Museum, and *Judith* is in the same MS. The Exeter Book is in the library of Exeter Cathedral, and was placed there by Bishop Leofric in 1071. It contains the *Riddles*, the *Elegies*, the *Crist*, the *St Guthlac*, the *Phœnix*, the *Juliana*, the *Widsith*, the *Complaint of Deor*, and other poems. It is a kind of anthology. The Vercelli Book, found at Vercelli in 1822, contains, interspersed among homilies, the *Andreas*, the *Fates of the Apostles*, the *Dream of the Rood*, the *Elene*, and two unimportant poems. The *Junian* MS. of the so-called Cædmonian poems is in the Bodleian. The *Fight at Finnsburg* was found on the cover of a MS. of Homilies at Lambeth, *Waldhere* on two vellum leaves at Copenhagen ; the *Battle of Brunanburh* is in the Anglo-Saxon Chronicle, and the *Battle of Maldon* in a copy of the original MS. made by Hearne. Only one MS. of each of these poems exists.

Of Ælfred's translations we have many MSS.—three of the *Cura Pastoralis*, five of *Bæda's History*, two of the *Orosius*, two of the *De Consolatione*, four of the *Laws*. The *Soliloquia* are in the MS. containing *Beowulf.* Of Ælfric's works there are many MSS. Seven MSS. of the *English Chronicle* exist. MS. A, the Parker MS. written at Winchester, is at Cambridge ; MS. B is at the British Museum, and was made at Canterbury ; MS. C is at the British Museum, and is an Abingdon MS. ; MS. D, also at the Museum, is the Worcester Chronicle ; MS. E, now at the Bodleian (the Laud MS.), was done at Peterborough ; MS. F, at the British Museum, was probably kept at Canterbury ; MS. G, also probably kept at Canterbury, is at the British Museum, and is likely to be a copy of MS. A.

[When Modern English was beginning to show its full powers in the hands of the early Elizabethan writers, the oldest stage of the tongue was almost forgotten, save for the little knowledge required by those whose business it was to spell out and interpret Anglo-Saxon charters and the like. At the Reformation Anglo-Saxon religious literature was looked up for controversial purposes; Archbishop Parker gathered and edited MSS., and greatly promoted 'Saxon' studies. Verstegen shows he knew some Anglo-Saxon in his *Restitution of Decayed Intelligence in Antiquities* (1606); and Spelman was driven to make his *Glossarium* (Part I. 1626) by the difficulties he met in studying our oldest laws. Francis Junius, or Du Jon, a Continental Protestant who settled in England in 1621, devoted himself to the study of Anglo-Saxon and the cognate Teutonic tongues, edited the so-called Cædmon and other Old English books, and gave his name to the Junian MS. Hickes, the nonjuring bishop, published the first edition of his Anglo-Saxon and Mœso-Gothic Grammar in 1689; and all students of early English history owe a debt of gratitude to Thomas Hearne, 'who studied and preserved antiquities.' Percy in his *Reliques* takes no cognisance of the oldest poetry. Warton's *History of English Poetry* (vol. i. 1774) professedly begins with the close of the tenth century; but what he says by way of introduction on the three successive 'dialects of Saxon'—British Saxon (till the Danish occupation), Danish Saxon ('British Saxon corrupted by the Danes'), and Norman Saxon ('Danish Saxon adulterated with French')—shows how far he was to seek in this field; 'the spurious Cædmon's beautiful poetical paraphrase of the Book of Genesis' he names as written in Danish Saxon. Gray's knowledge of Icelandic and his interest in Welsh poetry and in 'Ossian' make it certain that, had he carried out his projected *History of Poetry*, the section on what he called 'the introduction of the poetry of the Goths into these islands by the Saxons and Danes' would have received fuller attention than heretofore. Vicesimus Knox's *Elegant Extracts* (first of many editions, 1783) does not include this period within its scope. The first edition of Ellis's *Specimens of the Early English Poets* (1790) has nothing earlier than Surrey and Wyatt; but the 1801 edition gives not only Middle English poems, but the old song of Brunanburh, with a literal translation, and the ingenious rendering made by Hookham Frere, when an Eton schoolboy, into Rowley-like fourteenth-century English. In the notes Ellis accepts for Anglo-Saxon words derivations from 'Chaldaic' and Latin as unhesitatingly as from 'Gothic.' Rask the Dane put the study on a sounder philological footing by his Grammar (1817), which Thorpe translated; and the works of Thorpe, Bosworth, and Kemble in the first half of the century revived in the English people interest in their old language and literature. Conybeare's *Specimens of Anglo-Saxon Poetry* appeared in 1826. Campbell begins his *Specimens of the British Poets* (7 vols. 1819) with Chaucer and the *King's Quair;* and in the earlier issues and reprints of this Cyclopædia (1844–74) Anglo-Saxon literature was dismissed in less than three pages.

For further study the reader may be referred to *English Literature from the Beginning to the Norman Conquest* (1898), by the writer of the preceding section of this work, Dr Stopford A. Brooke, or to his *History of Early English Literature* (2 vols. 1892), which describes and appreciates still more fully the whole of the Anglo-Saxon

Lightning Source UK Ltd.
Milton Keynes UK
UKOW06f1923040815

256385UK00014B/328/P